HOTSPOTS
ORLAN

Written by Lindsay and Pete Bennett, updated by Ryan Levitt

Published by Thomas Cook Publishing
A division of Thomas Cook Tour Operations Limited.
Company registration no. 1450464 England
The Thomas Cook Business Park, Unit 9, Coningsby Road,
Peterborough PE3 8SB, United Kingdom
Email: books@thomascook.com, Tel: + 44 (0)1733 416477
www.thomascookpublishing.com

Produced by Cambridge Publishing Management Limited
Burr Elm Court, Main Street, Caldecote CB23 7NU

ISBN 13: 978-1-84157-974-0

First edition © 2006 Thomas Cook Publishing
This second edition © 2008
Text © Thomas Cook Publishing,
Maps © Thomas Cook Publishing/PCGraphics (UK) Limited

Project Editor: Karen Fitzpatrick
Production/DTP: Steven Collins

Printed and bound in Spain by GraphyCems

Cover photography © Alamy/Tony Craddock

CONTENTS

INTRODUCTION 5
Getting to know Orlando.............8
The best of Orlando....................10
Symbols key 12

RESORTS & THEME PARKS 13
International Drive.......................15
Lake Buena Vista.........................26
Kissimmee.....................................29
Maingate.......................................35
Celebration 37
Walt Disney World® Resort........41
   Magic Kingdom® Park..........42
   Epcot®.....................................46
   Disney's Animal
   Kingdom® Park 50
   Disney's Hollywood™
   Studios...................................52
   Best of the rest.....................54
   Downtown Disney®...............56
Universal Orlando Resort® 59
   Universal Studios Florida® ...60
   Islands of Adventure®..........65
   Universal CityWalk®..............71
SeaWorld®....................................73
Discovery Cove®..........................77

EXCURSIONS 81
Busch Gardens®...........................83
Beach resorts 89

Fantasy of Flight...........................91
NASA Kennedy Space Center.....92
Silver Springs® 96
St Augustine 98
St Petersburg 100

LIFESTYLE 101
Food & drink...............................102
Menu decoder 104
Shopping.....................................105
Children.......................................106
Sports & activities......................107
Festivals & events 108

PRACTICAL INFORMATION ...109
Accommodation 110
Preparing to go...........................112
During your stay.........................115

INDEX 125

MAPS
Florida...6
International Drive 14
International Drive detail 18
Kissimmee......................................28
Celebration....................................38
Disney Resorts...............................40
Excursions......................................82

WHAT'S IN YOUR GUIDEBOOK?

Independent authors Impartial, up-to-date information from our travel experts who meticulously source local knowledge.

Experience Thomas Cook's 165 years in the travel industry and guidebook publishing enriches every word with expertise you can trust.

Travel know-how Contributions by thousands of staff around the globe, each one living and breathing travel.

Editors Travel-publishing professionals, pulling everything together to craft a perfect blend of words, pictures, maps and design.

You, the traveller We deliver a practical, no-nonsense approach to information, geared to how you really use it.

● *Orlando: city of dreams*

INTRODUCTION
Getting to know Orlando

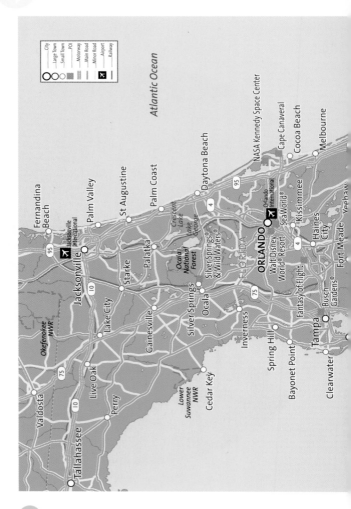

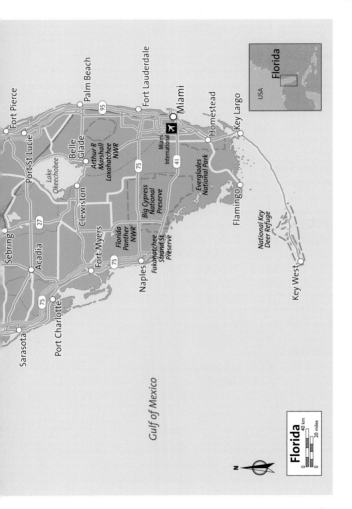

Getting to know Orlando

WHERE IS IT?
Orlando sits at the centre of Florida, a narrow finger of land on America's east coast, extending south-east towards the Caribbean Sea; Key West, Florida's southernmost city, sits just 144 km (90 miles) north of Havana, Cuba. Orlando is only 75 km (47 miles) away from the east coast, 160 km (100 miles) from the west coast. Florida is a very flat state, with the highest point only 23 m (75 ft) above sea level.

THEME PARKS
Without Walt Disney, there would be no Orlando as we know it today. He bought up acres of swampland in order to create his **Magic Kingdom® Park**. When visitor numbers exploded, other parks followed, and now Orlando is the best place in the world to let your imagination run riot. With the help of 100 cartoon characters, the best ride designers in the world and film gurus like Steven Spielberg lending a hand, it is easy to see why everything is so expertly done.

With the addition of Aquatica in 2008, there are now eight major parks, where you can spend at least one whole day each, not to mention a host of other attractions that would be major pulls elsewhere. Of its kind, this is top-notch entertainment.

SHOPPING
Orlando has become a shopping mecca for many tourists because the brand names are international, the quality of goods is high, and prices are low, especially for consumer goods such as clothing, electronics and designer items.

CLIMATE
With a temperature that rarely drops below 22–24°C (the low 70s°F) in the daytime, Orlando is a place where you can enjoy sunshine year-round. Even Orlando's rain is warm. Summer temperatures average 35°C (the 90s°F), though summer days can be dotted by rain showers.

⬤ Top-name labels are available on International Drive

THE BEST OF ORLANDO

Having fun is what Orlando is all about. Whether you're young or simply young-at-heart, these top attractions and experiences are sure to satisfy:

TOP 10 ATTRACTIONS

- **Daytona Beach driving** Cruise along the Oceanside on Daytona's sands in your dune buggy or hot rod for an experience to remember (see pages 89–90).

- **Discovery Cove®** Probably the best place on earth to swim with dolphins. The passion of the trainers for the animals is beyond compare (see pages 77–80).

- **Disney's Hollywood™ Studios** See how films are made on the informative backlot tour or simply experience chills and thrills in the Twilight Zone Tower of Terror™ (see pages 52–3).

- **Downtown Disney®** And you thought Disney was just for the kids! This complex of nightclubs, restaurants and shopping is just for grown-ups (see pages 56–8).

- **Epcot®** Take a trip around the planet by visiting the various national pavilions and enjoy the World Showcase (see pages 46–9).

- **Gatorland®** Home to hundreds of alligators. These prehistoric creatures are truly a sight to behold (see page 30).

- **Magic Kingdom® Park** The place where it all began – dreams come true under Cinderella's Castle. Younger kids love the land that Mickey built (see pages 42–5).

- **NASA Kennedy Space Center** From the magic of Mickey to the magic of outer space. Explore the place where dreams take flight and astronauts head for the stars (see pages 92–5).

- **SeaWorld®** Watch animals perform with their dedicated trainers and learn about conserving the creatures in our oceans too (see pages 73–6).

- **Universal Studios Florida®** A celebration of some of the world's favourite films is combined with fantastic thrill rides and a cute section dedicated to the cartoons of Hanna-Barbera for the perfect theme park (see pages 60–4).

🔽 *Catch the action at Disney's Hollywood™ Studios* © Disney

SYMBOLS KEY
The following symbols are used throughout this book:

ⓐ address ☏ telephone ⓦ website address ⓔ email
🕑 opening times ❶ important

The following symbols are used on the maps:

𝒊 information office		⭕	city
✉ post office		⭕	large town
🏠 shopping		◯	small town
✈ airport		◼	POI (point of interest)
➕ hospital		═	motorway
🛡 police station		—	main road
🚌 bus station		—	minor road
🚆 railway station		—	railway
✝ church			

❶ numbers denote featured cafés, restaurants & evening venues

RESTAURANT CATEGORIES
The symbol after the name of each restaurant listed in this guide
indicates the price of a typical three-course meal without drinks.
£ = up to $10   ££ = $10–$25   £££ = over $25

▶ *Cavorting killer whales: a highlight at SeaWorld®*

RESORTS & THEME PARKS
Places under the sun

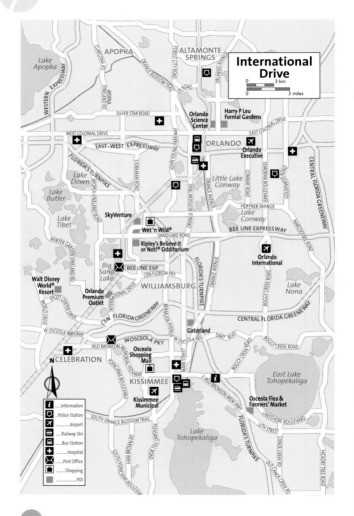

International Drive

International Drive

The original resort centre of Orlando, International Drive, known to everyone as I-Drive, is still the fastest-growing tourist venue in the city. It has hundreds of restaurants, a choice of hotels for every budget, great shopping, and a range of inexpensive things to do, which means that you don't have to head to the major theme parks to fill your day. This is the best place to stay in Orlando if you do not want to hire a car. I-Drive is within easy reach of all the major parks by taxi, and some hotels provide courtesy transfer buses.

THINGS TO SEE & DO

Congo River Adventure Golf

Congo River now has two I-Drive locations to choose from and goes one better than its many competitors by offering prizes for great rounds. Plus, there are live alligators (small ones) you can feed.
ⓐ 6312 International Drive (ⓣ 407 352 0042) and 5901 International Drive (ⓣ 407 248 9181) ⓦ www.congoriver.com ⓛ 10.00–23.00 Sun–Thur, 10.00–midnight Fri & Sat ❶ Admission charge

Harry P Leu Formal Gardens

Take a break from the frenetic pace of Orlando with a visit to the serene former estate of business tycoon Harry Leu. The Leus were horticulture buffs who travelled the world, taking snippings back for their garden. The result is America's largest camellia collection outside California, a palm and bamboo garden, and Florida's largest formal rose garden.
ⓐ 1920 N. Forest Ave, Orlando ⓣ 407 246 2620 ⓦ www.leugardens.org
ⓛ 09.00–17.00 daily except Christmas

Helicopter tours

Air tours around Orlando, starting with a mini-tour along the southerly section of I-Drive. You can take trips over some of the theme parks, especially thrilling at dusk when the nightly firework displays are underway.

● *Get Wet 'n Wild® in Orlando*

The ultimate tour takes you along the same flight path that the space shuttle uses when it lands at Cape Canaveral Air Force Base.
Air Florida Helicopters ⓐ 8990 International Drive ❶ 407 354 1400
🕙 10.00–19.00 Sun–Thur, 10.00–21.00 Fri & Sat

Magical Midway

This is the nearest thing to a fairground complex on I-Drive. Magical Midway features an unusual elevated go-cart track, along with bumper cars and bumper boats with water pistols to wet your fellow riders and even passers-by on the street. Refreshments are also available in the complex.

ⓐ 7001 International Drive ⓣ 407 370 5353 ⓛ Daily, but times vary according to the season

Orlando Science Center

If you're travelling with children, a visit to this world-class science museum should not be missed; films in the Planetarium are a treat, and the exhibits first rate.

ⓐ 777 East Princeton Street ⓣ 407 514 2000 ⓦ www.osc.org
ⓛ 09.00–17.00 Tue–Thur, 09.00–21.00 Fri & Sat, 12.00–17.00 Sun
ⓘ Admission charge

The Peabody Ducks

Ducks are mascots at the Peabody Hotel and a small group are kept in five-star luxury in a special duck-friendly room on an upper floor. Every day at 11.00 the ducks are escorted down to the lobby by a liveried chaperone, to swim in the fountain of the hotel lobby. They make their way back into the lift at 17.00.

ⓐ The Peabody Hotel, 9801 International Drive ⓣ 407 352 4000
ⓦ www.peabodyorlando.com

Pirate's Cove Adventure Golf

A tropical pirate's hideout is the theme for these two mini-golf courses.

ⓐ 8501 International Drive ⓣ 407 352 7378 ⓛ 09.00–23.30 daily
ⓘ Admission charge

Ripley's Believe It or Not!® Odditorium

Robert Ripley is famed in America as an explorer and collector of strange and wonderful things. His museums are filled with the kind of exhibits that make youngsters squeal and squirm and where parents are bombarded with questions they cannot answer. Here, you will find a full-scale model 1907 Rolls-Royce made out of matchsticks and a grain of rice decorated with a beautifully painted sunset.

ⓐ 8201 International Drive ⓣ 407 363 4418 ⓛ 09.00–01.00 daily
ⓘ Admission charge

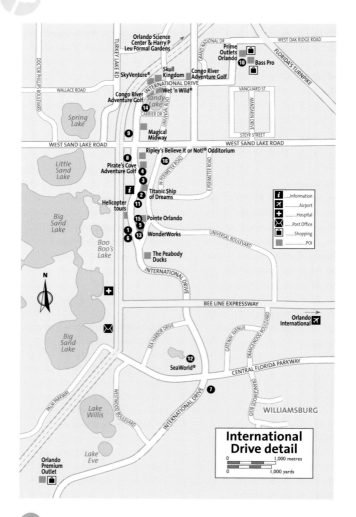

Orlando Science Center & Harry P Leu Formal Gardens

WEST OAK RIDGE ROAD

GRAND NATIONAL DR

Prime Outlets Orlando

Bass Pro

FLORIDA'S TURNPIKE

TURKEY LAKE RD

DOCTOR PHILLIPS BOULEVARD

SkyVenture®

Skull Kingdom

Congo River Adventure Golf

WALLACE ROAD

VANGUARD ST

INTERNATIONAL DRIVE

Congo River Adventure Golf

Wet 'n Wild®

Sandy Lake

CARRIER DR

14

MANDAN DRIVE

Spring Lake

9

STEYR STREET

Magical Midway

WEST SAND LAKE ROAD

WEST SAND LAKE ROAD

8

Little Sand Lake

Ripley's Believe It or Not!® Odditorium

16

Pirate's Cove Adventure Golf

4

3

W PERIMETER ROAD

E PERIMETER ROAD

i

Big Sand Lake

2

Titanic Ship of Dreams

Helicopter tours

11

15

Pointe Orlando

5

i ....Information
✈ ....Airport
✚ ....Hospital
✉ ....Post Office
🛍 ....Shopping
■ ....POI

1

13

6

WonderWorks

UNIVERSAL BOULEVARD

Boo Boo's Lake

N

The Peabody Ducks

INTERNATIONAL DRIVE

✚

BEE LINE EXPRESSWAY

Orlando International ✈

Big Sand Lake

✉

SEA HARBOR DRIVE

GATEWAY AVENUE

ORANGEWOOD BOULEVARD

12

SeaWorld®

CENTRAL FLORIDA PARKWAY

ORANGEWOOD BLVD

Lake Willis

WESTWOOD BLVD

INTERNATIONAL DRIVE

7

WILLIAMSBURG

PALM PARKWAY

International Drive detail

0 .... 1,000 metres
0 .... 1,000 yards

Lake Eve

Orlando Premium Outlet

🛍

Skull Kingdom

You have to walk through the gaping mouth of a skull to get to the ticket office of this medieval-style castle attraction. Once inside you will journey through ghoulish corridors, rooms and mazes with robotic monsters, a blood-curdlingly scary soundtrack and a few real-life shocks around every corner. This is a really effective development of the old haunted house attraction.

ⓐ 5933 American Way (at intersection with International Drive)
ⓣ 407 354 1564 ⓦ www.skullkingdom.com ⓛ 11.00–22.00 daily
ⓘ Admission charge

SkyVenture®

Want to feel the sensation of skydiving without having to jump out of an aeroplane? Soar on a cushion of moving air and feel the sensation of free-fall while just a few feet off the floor. Training is given. Not suitable for children under eight.

ⓐ 6805 Visitors Circle (opposite Wet 'n Wild®) International Drive
ⓣ 407 903 1150 ⓦ www.skyventure.com ⓛ 10.00–24.00 daily
ⓘ Admission charge, reservations recommended

Titanic Ship of Dreams – The Exhibition

Plunge into the world of the *Titanic* on its final voyage. This claims to be the first interactive attraction in the world and features genuine artefacts from the vessel itself. Recreations of the ship's interior make you feel that you are there and actors play the parts of passengers on that long, final night. You will really begin to understand the terror and despair that all those on board must have felt.

ⓐ 8445 International Drive ⓣ 407 248 1166
ⓦ www.titanicshipofdreams.com ⓛ 10.00–22.00 daily
ⓘ Admission charge

Wet 'n Wild®

Orlando's original water park, Wet 'n Wild® stays ahead of the rest with enough to keep the family occupied all day. The water chutes and wave pools remain eternally popular, as is the **The Storm**, an enclosed slide filled with atmospheric thunder and lightning, and the **Lazy River** – bobbing along in a giant inner tube. **The Black Hole** calls for a little more courage as riders are carried along a long, dark, twisting, water-filled tunnel, with the ultimate test of vertical body-slides 23 m (75 ft) high. Women should consider wearing a one-piece swimming costume here – the water rides can dislodge even the best-fitting bikinis!

ⓐ 6200 International Drive ⓣ 407 351 1800 ⓦ www.wetnwild.com
ⓛ Daily, but times vary according to season ❶ Admission charge

WonderWorks

You can't miss the WonderWorks building as you travel down I-Drive. The whole façade is upside down and the story is that this building has been ripped up by a hurricane and landed on its roof, complete with sections of pavement and palm trees! Once inside, WonderWorks offers a collection of over 80 high-tech interactive exhibits that will surprise and enthrall visitors of all ages. These include 'swimming with sharks'

🔺 *WonderWorks: how did that happen?*

and what it feels like to be in an earthquake. The top floor is one vast arena where you can play laser tag (separate ticket).

🅐 9067 International Drive, Pointe Orlando Mall 🅣 407 351 8800
🅦 www.wonderworksonline.com 🅛 09.00–24.00 daily
🅘 Admission charge

TAKING A BREAK

Restaurants & bars (*see map on page 18*)

Sizzlers £ ❶   An exceptionally good-value eatery where you order and pay at reception, before heading to your seat to wait for your food. The buffet items are excellent, steaks done the way you ask for them and all the entrées are cooked fresh. Good food without the frills.
🅐 9142 International Drive 🅣 407 351 5369 🅛 07.00–23.00 daily

Bahama Breeze ££ ❷   One of the few places on I-Drive where you can eat outside on their deck. Snacks include Mexican, Cuban and Thai dishes and the full menu features meat and seafood options. Live reggae and Caribbean music nightly. 🅐 8849 International Drive 🅣 407 248 2499 🅛 16.00–01.00 daily 🅘 You must be over 21 to be on the deck after 21.00 or be accompanied by an adult

Boston Lobster Feast ££ ❸   Just as the name suggests, it is seafood and lobster all the way here, including an all-inclusive-price seafood buffet that seems more popular than the à la carte menu. 🅐 8731 International Drive (four blocks north of the Convention Center) 🅣 407 248 8606
🅦 www.bostonlobsterfeast.com 🅛 17.00–22.00 daily

Café TuTu Tango ££ ❹   Bohemian, colourful tapas eatery that's good for families with fussy eaters. Kids will love being able to select lots of different dishes – each explained in succulent detail by the friendly, efficient and knowledgeable waiting staff. 🅐 8625 International Drive
🅣 407 248 2222 🅦 www.cafetututango.com 🅛 11.30–23.00 Sun–Thur, 11.30–01.00 Fri & Sat

Dan Marino's Town Tavern ££ ❺ A great sports bar and restaurant owned by footballing legend Dan Marino. Drop in for a drink and bar snack or full meal. Menu includes steaks, chicken dishes, burgers and salads. ⓐ At Pointe Orlando, 9101 International Drive ❶ 407 363 1013 Ⓦ www.danmarinosrestaurant.com ⓛ 11.00–23.00 daily

Ming Court ££ ❻ Chinese food done very well at this excellent establishment offering tasty Chinese-American treats. Children get their own menu offering American classics with an Asian twist. ⓐ 9188 International Drive ❶ 407 351 9988 Ⓦ www.ming-court.com ⓛ 11.00–14.30, 16.30–23.30 daily

Thai Thani ££ ❼ A very good Thai restaurant with a lovely atmosphere. The menu even includes a full sushi bar. ⓐ 11025 International Drive ❶ 407 239 9733 Ⓦ www.thaithani.net ⓛ 11.00–22.00 daily

Ran Getsu of Tokyo £££ ❽ Relax in the elegant, yet traditional outdoor gardens of this high-class Japanese establishment that is always a favourite with Asian tourists. On Thursday, Friday and Saturday evenings, there's a Japanese drum show to accompany the delicious dishes. ⓐ 8400 International Drive ❶ 407 345 0044 Ⓦ www.rangetsu.com ⓛ 17.00–23.30 daily

Ronnie's Steak House £££ ❾ A refined steak house with fine cigars and a reasonable wine list. ⓐ 7500 International Drive (free shuttle bus in I-Drive area) ❶ 407 313 3000 ⓛ 16.00–22.00 daily, happy hour 17.00–20.00 ❶ Reservations recommended

AFTER DARK

Cinemark Festival Bay ❿ At the top of I-Drive near Prime Outlets Orlando, this cinema has 20 screens, perfect to fill the odd wet evening. ⓐ 5150 International Drive ❶ 407 351 3317 Ⓦ www.cinemark.com ⓛ 10.00–22.00 daily

Howl at the Moon ⓫ A cheesy romp of a duelling piano bar, in new digs. ⓐ 8815 International Drive ⓣ 407 354 5999 ⓦ www.howlatthemoon.com ⓘ Admission charge

Makahiki Luau at SeaWorld® ⓬ SeaWorld® stays open until late in summer and the shows always finish with an impressive firework display. Perhaps the most spectacular show is the Aloha Polynesian Luau, with live music, dancing and tropical dinner. ⓣ 407 351 3600 ⓛ Daily at 18.30 in summer ⓘ Admission charge (tickets sold separately from the general SeaWorld® admission)

Masters of Magic ⓭ A 90-minute high-energy show with grand illusions and tricks by Typhoon Lou and his team. Pizza and pop are available 45 mins before the show starts, or you can opt for the show only. ⓐ 8815 International Drive (near the Pointe Orlando mall) ⓣ 407 345 3456 ⓛ Shows Wed–Sun at 18.30 and 21.00 ⓘ Reservations recommended

Pirate's Dinner Adventure ⓮ Swashbuckling galore at one of the most child-interactive of the several dinner shows on offer. You are seated for dinner in a Spanish galleon and before long you are cheering for your hero and booing the rest. Afterwards there's a Buccaneer's Bash with disco music and fun dances. A five-course meal (including pre-show appetisers and drinks) is included in the price. ⓐ 6400 Carrier Drive (off International Drive behind Wet 'n Wild®) ⓣ 407 206 5100 ⓦ www.piratesdinneradventure.com ⓛ Daily from 18.30 (show starts at 20.00) ⓘ Admission charge

Pointe Orlando ⓯ There is live music most nights at the upper level of this shopping mall, where most of the restaurants are situated. **XS**, within the mall, has over 100 interactive games and simulators, and it is also a popular nightclub. The **Muvico Cinema complex** has 21 screens. ⓐ 9101 International Drive ⓣ 407 248 2838 ⓦ www.pointeorlando.com ⓛ 10.00–22.00 Mon–Sat, 11.00–21.00 Sun ⓘ Admission charge to clubs

🔺 *Shopping on I-Drive is fun for all the family*

Sleuth's Merry Mystery Dinner Shows ⓰ Think Cluedo on stage and you have the essence of this entertaining dinner show. If you solve the murder you win a prize. Three theatres and several different murder plots keep the acting fresh. ⓐ 8267 Universal Boulevard ⓣ 407 363 1985 or 800 393 1985 (freephone in US) ⓦ www.sleuths.com ⓛ Nightly 19.30 ⓘ Admission charge

SHOPPING

I-Drive offers some of the best bargain tourist shopping in Orlando. You will find plenty of lower-priced souvenirs on sale, including many with a Disney theme – but watch the quality, as this varies greatly.

Bass Pro shops: Outdoor World The place to come for your outdoor and tropical clothing, fishing gear and camping supplies. Very reasonable prices. 🅐 5156 International Drive ☎ 407 563 5200 🅦 www.basspro.com 🕐 09.00–21.00 Mon–Sat, 11.00–16.00 Sun

Orlando Premium Outlet An excellent mall, technically in Lake Buena Vista, but the outlet is just off I-Drive (south of the main tourist area) and linked to it by an I-Ride route. Prices for designer line ends and slight seconds are up to 40 per cent lower than the US high street – offering visitors an even greater saving. 🅐 8200 Vineland Avenue ☎ 407 238 7787 🅦 www.premiumoutlets.com 🕐 10.00–22.00 daily

Pointe Orlando The newest shopping and entertainment area on I-Drive with stores such as Banana Republic, Abercrombie & Fitch, and other high street names. 🅐 9101 International Drive ☎ 407 248 2838 🕐 10.00–22.00 Mon–Sat, 11.00–21.00 Sun

Prime Outlets Orlando Comprises what is also often referred to as the Belz Outlet Malls – more than 170 high-street-style shops which offer significant savings on overstocked items from retailers including Gap, Levi's, Eddie Bauer and scores more. Locals drive from miles around – it's not just tourists. There are two campuses. 🅐 5401 W Oak Ridge Road 🅐 5211 International Drive (at the northern end) ☎ 407 352 9611 🅦 www.primeoutlets.com 🕐 All stores open Mon–Sat 10.00–21.00, Sun 10.00–18.00

Lake Buena Vista

Walt Disney wanted to keep as much hotel business for himself as he could, within Disney's gates. The lower prices of hotels at nearby Lake Buena Vista cemented the city's popularity. That's still true, and while there's not much else here, with a rental car you quickly get to the parks or Orlando for an evening on the town.

THINGS TO SEE & DO

Pirate's Cove Adventure Golf
Pit your wits against 36-hole courses, through caves, over footbridges and under waterfalls.
ⓐ Crossroads Mall ☎ 407 827 1242 🕙 09.00–23.30 daily
❶ Admission charge

TAKING A BREAK

Bahama Breeze £–££ This Caribbean-style bar/restaurant has an open terrace. You can dine or have drinks and listen to live reggae music. Great atmosphere after dark. Age restriction on the terrace after 21.00.
ⓐ 8735 Vineland Avenue ☎ 407 938 9010 🕙 16.00–01.00 daily

Hooters £–££ A great range of dishes from chicken wings and onion rings to burgers, fish sandwiches and salads all served in informal fashion by the Hooters girls in their skimpy uniforms (be warned if you're bringing children). ⓐ 8510 Palm Parkway ☎ 407 239 0900 🕙 11.00–24.00 daily

Tony Roma's ££ A great place for slightly smarter family dining, Tony Roma's concentrates on ribs (served with their signature BBQ sauce) but also serves a range of dishes including steak, chicken and seafood platters. ⓐ 12167 South Apopka-Vineland Road ☎ 407 239 8040
ⓦ www.tonyromas.com 🕙 11.00–23.00 Sun–Thur, 11.00–24.00 Fri & Sat

California Grill ££–£££ High-end Californian and American cuisine with light seafood and vegetarian specialities and a great view of the Disney nightly fireworks. ⓐ 4600 North World Drive ① 407 939 3463 ⏱ 17.30–23.00 daily

The Crab House ££–£££ The menu leans heavily towards seafood, particularly Maine lobster and excellent crabs, but non-fish lovers can also choose from a range of chicken, steak and pasta. ⓐ 8496 Palm Parkway ① 407 239 1888 ⏱ 11.30–22.30 daily

SHOPPING

Lake Buena Vista has a number of small open-air malls, including **Palm Parkway**, **Shoppes at Vista Center** and **Crossroads of Lake Buena Vista**. These shopping centres have a range of shops, but by no means the selection available on I-Drive, although Crossroads (① 407 827 7300 ⏱ 10.00–22.00 daily) is convenient for Downtown Disney® Marketplace, where there is a good choice of genuine Disney souvenirs.

Bargain World and **Athlete's Foot** Two large bargain sports stores. ⓐ On the main State Road 535, also called Vineland/Apopka Road, which cuts through the resort ⏱ 10.00–21.00 Mon–Sat, 10.00–18.00 Sun

Orlando Premium Outlet Hugo Boss, Giorgio Armani, Tommy Hilfiger and Calvin Klein at discount prices (see page 25). ⓐ 8200 Vineland Avenue ① 407 238 7787

Lake Buena Vista also has one large outlet mall, **Lake Buena Vista Factory Stores**, with a range of designer names at outlet prices. ⓐ 15591 S Apopka-Vineland Rd (on the east side of I-4) ① 407 238 9301 ⓦ www.lbvfs.com ⏱ 10.00–21.00 Mon–Sat, 10.00–18.00 Sun

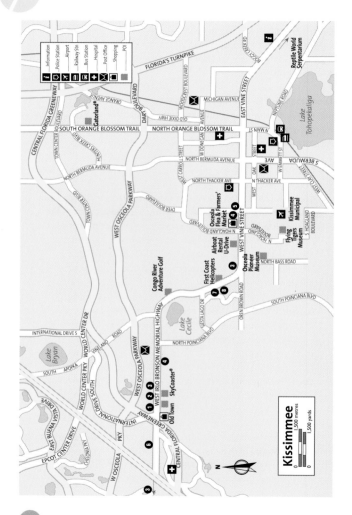

Kissimmee

Kissimmee

The city of Kissimmee's main drag, Highway 192 (also known as Irlo Bronson Memorial Highway and Vine Street on various sections), comprises over 9.5 km (6 miles) of cheap hotels, restaurants and attractions. Highway 192 is so long that it's essential you check where your hotel is in relation to the main attractions. Some hotels offer transfers to the Disney/Universal theme parks, but it is best to have your own transport.

THINGS TO SEE & DO

Airboat Rental U-Drive

You can pilot your own airboat along the narrow creeks that cut through the tranquil and unspoilt wilderness around Kissimmee.

ⓐ 4266 West Vine Street ⓣ 407 847 3672 ⓦ www.airboatrentals.com
ⓛ 09.00–17.00 daily

Congo River Adventure Golf

Congo River Golf offers prizes for great rounds and has live alligators to gawk at.

ⓐ 4777 Highway 192 (mile marker 12) ⓣ 407 396 6900
ⓦ www.congoriver.com ⓛ 10.00–23.00 Sun–Thur, 10.00–24.00 Fri & Sat
ⓘ Admission charge

First Coast Helicopters

Various tours on offer.

ⓐ 4619 West Irlo Bronson Memorial Highway ⓣ 407 390 0111
ⓘ Two people minimum

Flying Tigers Warbird Air Restoration Museum

Aircraft lovers will feel right at home surrounded by World War II war planes in this family-run museum, where you can watch restoration work on a range of American, British and German planes and have all your questions answered by the knowledgeable guides. Get a tour or take the controls of a North American T-6 Texan (aka Harvard), the main training aircraft for US pilots in World War II.

ⓐ 233 North Hoagland Boulevard ⓣ 407 933 1942
ⓦ www.warbirdmuseum.com ⓒ 09.00–17.00 daily ❗ Admission charge

Gatorland®

Unless you are lucky enough to spot one in the wild, the best place to see alligators in Florida is Gatorland®. There are hundreds of alligators on show here, from 4.5 m (15 ft) monsters to 20 cm (8 inch) hatchlings. The natural lake behind the main pens has a population of native birds and more than a few free-swimming alligators. This gives you the chance to view these animals in as near to wild conditions as is possible. The park is also excellent value for money.

ⓐ 14501 Orange Blossom Trail ⓣ 407 855 5496 or 800 393 5297 (freephone in US) ⓦ www.gatorland.com ⓒ 09.00–17.00 daily
❗ Admission charge

Old Town

Kissimmee's rendition of old town America is one of the most relaxing places to shop but it also offers its fair share of entertainment. You will find eateries and a couple of bars, along with fairground rides for the kids, including a huge Ferris wheel and vintage carousel. Every Friday and Saturday is classic car day with the great 'finned' styling of 1950s Chevrolets and Cadillacs. Catch the action at the Friday Nite Cruise (vehicles from 1972 to 1987) from 17.00, and the Saturday Cruise, which is in the daytime, from 13.00, with an average of more than 300 cars made earlier than 1972. Thursday nights it is classic bikes – mostly Harley-Davidsons – and on average, more than 700 motorcycles attend! Visitors can chat to the owners and take some great pictures.

ⓐ 5770 West Irlo Bronson Memorial Highway (3 km/2 miles east of I-4 exit 25) ⓣ 407 396 4888 ⓦ www.old-town.com ⓒ Daily 10.00–21.00, bars open until 23.00

● Getting to grips with the 'gators'

Osceola County Historical Society and Pioneer Center Museum

This museum contains numerous pioneer artifacts, as well as a pristine eight acre nature reserve and a large picnic pavilion. You'll also find an 1898 'Cracker House', a 1900 general store, and a sugar cane mill on site.

ⓐ 750 North Bass Road, Kissimmee, FL 34746-6037 ❶ 407 396-8644
🕐 10.00–16.00 Thur–Sat; 12.00–16.00 Sun ❶ Admission charge

Reptile World Serpentarium

Reptile World provides most of the anti-venom serum that treats victims of snakebite in Florida. You can learn all about this fascinating process and watch snakes being 'milked' of their poison, but the serpentarium also has a great collection of non-venomous species and turtles and lizards for you to view.

ⓐ 5705 East Irlo Bronson Highway in St Cloud (34 km/21 miles east of I-4 junction 25) ❶ 407 892 6905 🕐 09.00–17.00 Tues–Sun
❶ Admission charge

SkyCoaster®

SkyCoaster® cranks your specially designed harness 90 m (300 ft) into the air, from where you pull your own ripcord to initiate a spectacular free-fall and long dramatic sway backwards and forwards as you are lowered gently to earth.

ⓐ 2850 Florida Plaza Boulevard (mile marker 9 off Highway 192, next to Old Town) ⓣ 407 397 2509 ⓛ 16.00–24.00 Mon–Fri, 12.00–24.00 Sat & Sun ⓘ Admission charge

TAKING A BREAK

Restaurants (*see map on page 28*)
Bennigan's £–££ ❶   A great informal family restaurant with a wide range of American dishes on the menu including burgers, salads and steaks. Also open for breakfast. ⓐ 5877 West Irlo Bronson Memorial Highway (mile marker 9) ⓣ 407 390 0687 ⓦ www.bennigans.com ⓛ 08.00–22.00 daily

Pacino's Italian Ristorante ££ ❷   Great American-Italian-style pasta, along with a wide choice of steaks and seafood. ⓐ 5795 West Irlo Bronson Memorial Highway ⓣ 407 396 8022 ⓦ www.pacinos.com ⓛ 11.00–24.00 daily

Ponderosa Steakhouse ££ ❸   Obviously steaks are what Ponderosa do best – they grill them over open flame – although there is plenty more on the menu, including a 'grand buffet' and some great breakfast options. There are three in town. ⓐ 4024, 5771, and 7598 West Irlo Bronson Memorial Highway ⓣ 407 846 3339/397 2100/396 7721 ⓦ www.ponderosa.com ⓛ All are open 07.00–23.00 daily

Red Lobster ££ ❹   A good family restaurant for seafood. The menu is varied, including options for kids and adults. Obviously lobster is the speciality, but shrimp and catch of the day are tasty too. For non-fish eaters they have steak, chicken and salads. There are two locations in

Kissimmee. ⓐ 4010 West Vine St (ⓣ 407 846 3513/5690) and 7780 West Irlo Bronson Memorial Highway (ⓣ 407 396 6997)
ⓦ www.redlobster.com ⓛ Both 11.00–22.00 Sun–Thur, 11.00–23.00 Fri & Sat

Tony Roma's ££ ⑤   Another Tony Roma's that concentrates on ribs (served with their signature BBQ sauce) but also serves a range of dishes including steak, chicken and seafood platters. ⓐ 3415 West Vine Street ⓣ 407 870 9299 ⓦ www.tonyromas.com ⓛ 11.00–23.00 Mon–Fri, 11.00–24.00 Sat & Sun

SHOPPING

Old Town (see pages 30–1) This sanitised version of old town America is well worth a look. Its approach is very low key, compared with Disney and Universal, but this is no bad thing. You will find great gifts here that you will not see elsewhere, with rarely a Disney souvenir in sight. Chief amongst them is Americana of all kinds, a surf shop for clothing and equipment, an Irish shop selling themed goods from mugs to CDs of Irish music, and a ghoulish joke shop. ⓐ 5770 West Irlo Bronson Memorial Highway (3 km/2 miles east of I-4 exit 25) ⓣ 407 396 4888 ⓛ Shops open 10.00–21.00 Mon–Sat, 10.00–18.00 Sun

Osceola Flea & Farmers' Market One of the largest true farmers' markets in the region, where you can mix with real local people from the surrounding countryside. This market is a combination of car boot sales, craft markets and produce markets, and it is certainly interesting to browse even if you do not intend to buy. ⓐ 2801 East Irlo Bronson Memorial Highway ⓣ 407 846 2811 ⓛ 08.00–17.00 Fri–Sun

AFTER DARK

Arabian Nights ❻ Voted the number-one dinner attraction by readers of the *Orlando Sentinel* newspaper, this is a great place for children. Many different themed acts from cowboy jamboree and square dancing to Broadway intermingle with the love story of Princess Sheherazade and Prince Khalid. ⓐ 6225 West Irlo Bronson Memorial Highway ⓣ 407 239 9223 ⓦ www.arabian-nights.com ⓛ Open from 17.30 daily (show starts 19.00) ⓘ Admission charge

Capone's Dinner & Show ❼ Enter the world of 1920s American prohibition where gangsters ruled the underworld and their molls spent all the loot. An entertaining evening featuring shoot-outs as well as some inter-mob rivalry. ⓐ 4740 West Irlo Bronson Memorial Highway ⓣ 407 397 2378 ⓦ www.alcapones.com ⓛ From 19.00 daily (show starts 19.30) ⓘ Admission charge

Medieval Times ❽ Travel back to a time when men wore chain mail and rode horses, and where honour was proved in contests of jousting, sword-fights, chivalry, agility and strength. This is a great show for all the family. There is a medieval village with numerous artisans to visit while you wait for the performance to start. The roasted meat dinner is hot so watch young children, and you don't get cutlery, so take moist wipes for those after-dinner sticky fingers. ⓐ 4510 West Irlo Bronson Memorial Highway ⓣ 407 396 1518 or 888 935 6878 (freephone in US) ⓦ www.medievaltimes.com ⓛ 18.30 Mon–Fri (show starts 19.30), 18.15 Sat & Sun (show starts 19.30) ⓘ Admission charge

Maingate

A part of Kissimmee, Maingate has expanded along the main 192 highway of I-4 junction 25 as the demand for tourist accommodation has grown. It takes its name from its proximity to the old Walt Disney World® Resort main gate, although it is not right on the doorstep. It is a few miles east of the main Kissimmee attractions (see pages 28–33).

THINGS TO SEE & DO

Bonanza Mini-Golf
The Prospector and Gold Nugget Courses are designed like a set of old mining works and there is a café on site if you want refreshment.
ⓐ 7761 West Irlo Bronson Memorial Highway ⓣ 407 396 7536
ⓛ 09.00–24.00 daily

Green Meadows Farm
If you find yourself here with younger kids, the Green Meadows Farm is certainly one of the area's more charming excursions; more than 300 animals roam freely, and kids can pet and hold many of them, including sheep, piglets, donkeys and cows, which can be milked. Horse rides and shows take place all day.
ⓐ 1368 South Poinciana Boulevard ⓣ 407 846 0770
ⓦ www.greenmeadowsfarm.com ⓛ Tours take place daily from 09.30 to 16.30, farm open until 17.30 ❶ Admission charge

World of Orchids
For plant lovers, World of Orchids is the perfect place to spend some quality time. These state-of-the-art hot-houses have one of the world's largest collections of this rare tropical flower. Over 2,000 specimens are set in different environments. You can also purchase blooms and have them shipped home.
ⓐ 2501 North Old Lake Wilson Road ⓣ 407 396 1887
ⓦ www.worldoforchids.com ⓛ 09.30–17.30 Tues–Sun

TAKING A BREAK

Angel's Diner and Bakery ££ You will see the adverts for Angel's lobster feast, but keep in mind that this restaurant/buffet serves just about every type of American food and astounding breakfasts – it's the place to take a family that can't agree on what to order. ⓐ 7300 West Irlo Bronson Memorial Highway (at the Holiday Inn) ① 407 397 1960 ⓛ 07.00–23.00 daily

Giordano's ££ This Italian restaurant specialises in the famous Chicago-style stuffed pizza, but you can also order a variety of pasta dishes, sandwiches and salads ⓐ 7866 West Irlo Bronson Memorial Highway ① 407 397 0044 ⓛ 11.00–23.30 daily

Outback Steakhouse ££ 'No rules, just right!' is the motto of this Australian-themed eatery. The menu centres on steaks and chicken, but you can get a range of snacks from chicken wings to sandwiches, plus that famed Aussie beer. ⓐ Formosa Gardens, 7804 West Irlo Bronson Memorial Highway ① 407 396 0017 ⓛ 15.30–22.30 Sun–Thur, 15.30–23.30 Fri & Sat

SHOPPING
Take a trip to **Formosa Gardens** (ⓐ West Irlo Bronson Memorial Highway, mile marker 4), Maingate's principal shopping centre. Although small, it has a select range of shops and restaurants.

Celebration

Truly a 'celebration' of small town America, the way it used to be.
This charming, modern settlement has a cosy downtown area designed
by Disney, with more than a few tributes to the 1950s. Less a resort
than a living community, the beautiful lakefront and small shops and
restaurants of the centre are surrounded by streets of panel-clad family
homes: it is probably the most relaxing place to stay in Orlando.

THINGS TO SEE & DO

Carriage rides
Take a carriage ride from the lakefront along the main street and view
the wonderful homes – no two are the same.
🕐 09.00–17.00 daily

Pedalo rides on the lake
Fun for adults and children alike, the pedalos allow you to take to the
water at your own pace.
🕐 09.00–17.00 daily

Strolling around the lake
Probably the most popular pastime in Celebration. Take your time and
say hello to everyone as you pass.

TAKING A BREAK

Herman's Ice Cream Shoppe £ ❶ A delightfully hokey take on an old-
fashioned diner/malt shop. ⓐ 671 Front Street ⓣ 407 566 1300
🕐 11.00–21.00 Sun–Thur, 11.00–22.00 Fri & Sat

Upper Crust £ ❷ Hand-tossed pizzas are the speciality of this New
York-style neighbourhood pizzeria. ⓐ 606 Market Street ⓣ 407 566 1221
🕐 11.00–21.00 Sun–Thur, 11.00–22.00 Fri & Sat

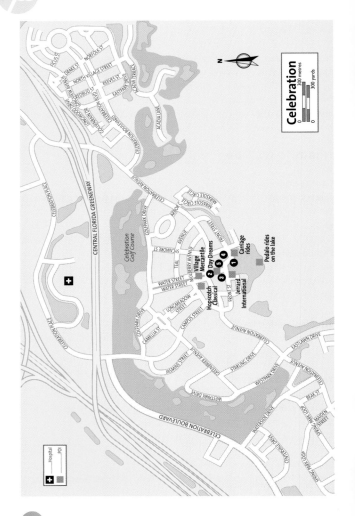

Celebration Town Tavern £££ ❸   The Town Tavern has a great reputation for New England seafood including lobster, chowder and fresh fish dishes. ⓐ 721 Front Street ⓣ 407 566 2526
ⓦ www.thecelebrationtowntavern.com ⓛ 11.00–15.00, 17.00–22.00 daily

Columbia Restaurant £££ ❹   A branch of one of Florida's oldest restaurants, Columbia serves Cuban/Spanish cuisine. It also has an excellent wine list, tapas bar and a cigar bar with fine Dominican cigars.
ⓐ 649 Front Street ⓣ 407 566 1505 ⓛ 11.30–22.00 daily

AFTER DARK

AMC Celebration Theater ❺   For the latest Hollywood releases.
ⓐ 651 Front Street ⓣ 407 566 1403 ⓛ 10.00–23.00 daily

SHOPPING
Shops in Celebration are scattered along the high street as you find in UK towns, but this is very unusual in the US. The merchandise is top class and generally pricey.
Day Dreams Collectable dolls and bears. ⓐ Mainstreet ⓣ 407 566 1231
Hopscotch Classical Ladies' clothes, shoes and accessories.
ⓐ Mainstreet ⓣ 407 566 2070
Jerrard International Home accessories from around the world.
ⓐ Lakefront ⓣ 407 566 2000
Village Mercantile Surfwear and accessories. ⓐ Market Street
ⓣ 407 566 0744

ⓐ Directions: I-4, exit 25A onto 192 East (Irlo Bronson Memorial Highway), right at the second set of lights ⓣ 407 566 4900 for information on all activities in the Celebration Marketplace
ⓛ All shops are open 10.00–21.00 Mon–Sat, 12.00–18.00 Sun

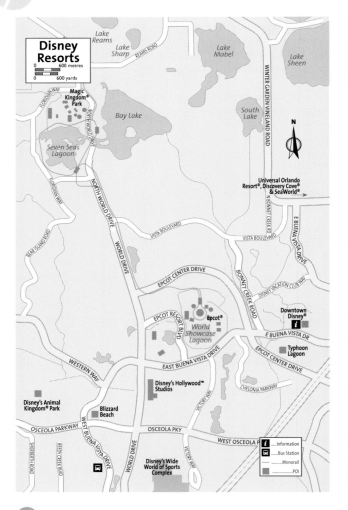

Walt Disney World® Resort

Walt Disney World® Resort put Orlando on the tourism map. It has developed far beyond the original plan, with four main parks and several other attractions as well as a range of themed hotels. Today it is almost a city within a city.

TICKET OPTIONS

Disney sells single tickets that are valid for one park, for one day. There is also a whole range of combined tickets that can save money.

Park Hopper tickets allow repeated access to the main parks for as long as the ticket is valid.

Park Hopper PLUS tickets give access to the four main parks and a number of other Disney attractions for as long as the ticket is valid. Unused Park Hopper days are still valid for your next visit to Walt Disney World® Resort.

Magic Your Way is a new family ticket option with several complex options of days and packages.

At the upper end of the ticketing options, the **World Pass** offers ten days' access to all parks, plus a character breakfast. Only the **Ultimate Park Hopper** ticket offers more choice, but you must stay at a Walt Disney World® Resort Hotel to be eligible to buy one.

MAKE THE MOST OF WALT DISNEY WORLD® RESORT

- Don't try to do too much. One park per day is a sensible strategy.
- Disney is hot and humid year round, and the danger of dehydration is real. Buy 1.5 litre water bottles, which you can refill (free) at any Disney restaurant. Drinks and water in the parks are expensive.
- Hire a pushchair (stroller) for infants because they will become tired.
- Use the FASTPASS system. Insert your ticket into the machine at the ride and it will give you a time to return, when you can go on the ride.
- For information on all Walt Disney World® Resort parks
  ❶ 407 824 4321 Ⓦ www.disneyworld.com

Magic Kingdom® Park

Magic Kingdom® Park, the original Disney park in the Walt Disney World® Resort, was Walt Disney's personal vision: bringing together the World of Disney® cartoons and good old-fashioned fantasy in a riot of colour, song and dance. The park is divided into seven different areas or 'lands'.

🔺 *Cinderella's Castle towers over Magic Kingdom® Park* © Disney

THINGS TO SEE & DO

Adventureland®

Hop aboard the **Jungle Cruise**, a journey through lush tropical forest where you will be able to spot wild animals and hidden temples. **Pirates of the Caribbean** highlights the Walt Disney Company's pioneering work with audio-animatronics – figures that move and talk. This exciting attraction is bursting with special effects. **The Magic Carpets of Aladdin** is a great ride for younger children, who will love the sensation of flying.

Fantasyland

If young children could design their own private playground, it would be Fantasyland. The **It's a Small World** ride probably sums up the appeal of the entire area. **Cinderella's Castle** is the towering symbol of Fantasyland, if not the whole of Magic Kingdom® Park. This abundance of towers and turrets is where the Princess herself presides over Cinderella's 'Surprise Celebration' show. Take to the skies in **Peter Pan's Flight** or **Dumbo the Flying Elephant**, ride through **Hundred-Acre Wood** at **The Many Adventures of Winnie the Pooh** or steer the giant teacups at the **Mad Tea Party** fairground ride.

Frontierland

Themed on the old Wild West, Frontierland has some of the most spectacular rides in Magic Kingdom® Park. **Splash Mountain®** is based on the 1946 Disney feature *Song of the South*, and is a journey through the land of Brer Rabbit. There is a grand finale – the clue's in the title! When you have dried off, head to **Big Thunder Mountain Railroad** – an exhilarating ride in an old carriage running out of control through an abandoned mineshaft.

Liberty Square

This is Disney's homage to post-independence USA. Most Americans make time for **The Hall of the Presidents** where audio-animatronic re-creations of every American leader tell their tale. Most non-Americans head to the 'ghoulish' surprises of the **Haunted Mansion**.

Main Street, USA®

Just beyond the Magic Kingdom® Park entrance, Main Street, USA® is one of the best vantage points for the daily **Disney Dreams Come True Parade**, where all your favourite Disney characters come out to entertain. There is a selection of shops and restaurants.

Mickey's Toontown Fair

This is the place to meet your favourite classic Disney characters 'in the flesh'. You will find Mr Mouse at home in **Mickey's Country House** and you can tour **Minnie's Country House**, decorated in her own distinctive style. **The Toontown Hall of Fame** brings you up close and personal with Goofy, Pluto and the rest of the gang.

Tomorrowland

Tomorrowland's appearance is a hi-tech contrast to the sugary pastels of Fantasyland. There is plenty to excite here, including **Space Mountain®**, a brilliant covered roller coaster ride that whizzes you across the universe. In **Buzz Lightyear's Space Ranger Spin**, the *Toy Story* character needs your help to win his battle against the evil Emperor Zurg. Older children will also enjoy **ExtraTERRORestrial Alien Encounter**. The **Galaxy Palace Theater** productions feature performances by a range of Disney characters.

TAKING A BREAK

Crystal Palace at Main Street, USA® ££ Meet Winnie the Pooh and Tigger too at this buffet restaurant. The children can help themselves, which takes the stress out of ordering.

Cinderella's Royal Table £££ At Cinderella's Castle in Fantasyland Cinderella presides over breakfast, lunch or dinner in the royal hall of her

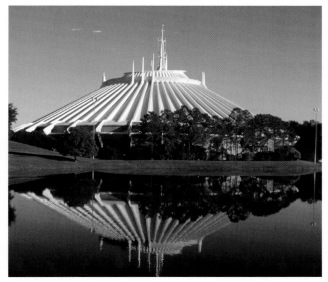

🔺 *Inside Space Mountain® you can travel the universe* © Disney

palace. Food 'fit for a king' includes steak, chicken, salads and seafood and is served by costumed waiting staff. ❶ Booking essential

AFTER DARK

SpectroMagic Parade
Takes place twice each night when the park opens late. The cast members' costumes are a mass of sparkling lights.

Wishes™ Nighttime Spectacular
Bringing the evening to a tumultuous end is the display when Cinderella's Castle lights up with a dazzling array of fireworks.

Epcot®

Epcot® stands for Experimental Prototype Community of Tomorrow. The park is divided into two separate areas. Future World offers the chance to experience themes such as the seas, energy and motion through interactive experiences. World Showcase offers a whistle-stop cultural tour around the planet via 11 country pavilions from all corners of the globe, including the UK, Italy and Japan. The food in this area is excellent.

Epcot® is probably the least impressive Disney park for younger children, because you do not meet a cartoon character around every corner and it is on a huge site. However, older children and adults will enjoy the educational content. Pick up an Epcot® guide map at the theme park entrance and time your day around 'must-see' shows. If you want to eat at one of the restaurants, make a reservation, as they can be fully booked by 10.00 during busy periods.

◆ *Spaceship Earth, Epcot®* © Disney

🔺 *Test Track at Future World* © Disney

THINGS TO SEE & DO

FUTURE WORLD
Imagination!
A theme park would not be a theme park without an exciting ride, so take time to enjoy **Honey, I Shrunk the Audience**, when you find yourself miniaturised by mad Professor Szalinski, alias Rick Moranis.

Innoventions: The Road to Tomorrow
Much of the technology that Disney has showcased in its two 'Innoventions' sections is now a part of everyday life. Nevertheless, you will still be astonished at what is coming around the corner.

The Land
Take a thought-provoking look at the environment with your hosts Pumbaa, Timon and Simba of *The Lion King* fame in 'Circle of Life'. This explores our relationship with the natural world around us.

The Seas with Nemo & Friends
A huge living coral reef where you can watch a whole ecosystem in action, from the tiniest plankton to the top marine predator, the shark. A new interactive area lets children speak with Crush – the turtle from *Finding Nemo*. Speaking of *Nemo*, kids will also love Bruce's Shark World.

Soarin'™
A hang-gliding journey above the rugged and fertile Californian landscape.

Spaceship Earth
The most photographed building at Future World, Spaceship Earth is a 50 m (164 ft) diameter geodesic dome (or golf ball). The spaceship explores human communication from cave paintings to hi-tech electronic messages.

Test Track
This is where you can explore the world of the motor car, how they are designed, built and tested – and of course how they are driven. You will be in the front seat on a gruelling and exhilarating simulated vehicle test.

Universe of Energy
Investigate the forces that have ruled our world since the beginning of time. This includes the chance to experience what an earthquake feels like.

Wonders of Life
The Wonders of Life pavilion explores how human beings work. Taking a simulator ride through the human bloodstream to the brain, lungs and heart on **Body Wars** is one of the highlights.

WORLD SHOWCASE
The American Adventure
The American Adventure is a joyous celebration of the country's history, depicted using amazing audio-animatronic figures.

Canada

Canada is the first realm if entering from the right side and features stunning vistas including recreations of the Rocky Mountains. The film *O Canada!* celebrates its wonderful varied landscape.

China

Explore China by viewing the spectacular 360° *Reflections of China* film or enjoy the seemingly impossible feats performed by the Dragon Legend Acrobats.

France

France lies in the shadow of a replica Eiffel Tower. The *Impressions of France* is excellent and of course the food is sublime.

Mexico

Mexico is housed in a recreation of a Mayan pyramid, where the **El Río del Tiempo** ride takes you on a journey through Mexican history.

Norway

This pavilion features the best ride in World Showcase – **Maelstrom**. You find yourself caught up in a North Sea storm.

TAKING A BREAK

The Sunshine Season Food Fair £ This is a selection of stalls which sell snacks from all the countries featured in World Showcase.

Coral Reef Restaurant £££ Enjoy your meal as sharks, rays and huge barracudas parade behind Plexiglas®.

AFTER DARK

IllumiNations: Reflections of Earth A riot of lasers, fireworks and music plays across the lake in a brilliant 15-minute climax to the day.

Disney's Animal Kingdom® Park

The success of the Disney film *The Lion King* sparked off the idea for this newest realm of the Disney family, where real, live animals from around the world are featured alongside rides and parades.

THINGS TO SEE & DO

Africa

This recreation of the vast African plains is the anchor for Disney's Animal Kingdom® Park. **Kilimanjaro Safaris®** allows you close encounters with elephants, giraffes and ostriches. Walk the **Pangani Forest Exploration Trail®** to see gorillas, or a hippo under water. Take the train to **Rafiki's Planet Watch®** for an introduction to wildlife conservation.

Asia

Step into the imaginary world of Anandapur and walk the **Maharajah Jungle Trek®** to meet gibbons and tapirs and view the king of Asian cats in their 2 ha (5 acre) **Tiger Range**. In the **Flights of Wonder** bird show, vultures, eagles and others show off their flying skills. Be prepared to get wet on **Kali River Rapids**. In **Expedition Everest**, you'll ride on a single-line track through Himalayan countryside. Look over the edge to see the 25 m (80 ft) drop!

Camp Minnie-Mickey

This is classic Walt Disney Theme Park stuff, with a series of Disney Character Greetings Trails. There is a spectacular stage extravaganza **Festival of the Lion King** and children will enjoy the **Pocahontas and Her Forest Friends** show.

DinoLand USA®

DinoLand has the park's most exciting ride, **Dinosaur** – asteroids fall from the skies and there is a T-Rex around every corner. At **The Boneyard®** children can climb life-size recreations of dinosaur skeletons and **Tarzan Rocks!** is a live concert featuring the best Disney film songs.

🔺 *Hurtle down the Forbidden Mountain in Expedition Everest* © Disney

Discovery Island®

At the heart of Disney's Animal Kingdom® Park is the 61 m (200 ft) tall **Tree of Life**, its trunk carved with hundreds of animals. You will find most of the restaurants and shops around it, along with **It's Tough to be a Bug!®** – a hilarious look at the world through an insect's eyes. You will also get a great view of **Mickey's Jammin' Jungle Parade**.

TAKING A BREAK

Rainforest Café® at the Oasis ££ An amazing restaurant that recreates a rainforest environment. Audio-animatronic animals add to the authentic effect. Menu includes steaks, chicken and sandwiches.

Disney's Hollywood™ Studios

Not just a theme park, but a real-life working film studio. Disney's Hollywood™ Studios takes you to the heart of the action, and provides some of the best rides of any of the Disney parks.

THINGS TO SEE & DO

Animation Courtyard

The Magic of Disney Animation gives this small area its name – a fascinating film exploring the art of cartoon making, with clips from many Disney classics. **Playhouse Disney – Live On Stage!** is a show for under-fives featuring characters from American TV. British children may not recognise many of them, but **Voyage of The Little Mermaid** brings the instantly recognisable Princess Ariel's world to life.

Behind the Scenes Tour

The Disney's Hollywood™ Studios Behind the Scenes Tour is a three-stage attraction where you get the chance to see how movies are made. **The Backstage Pass Tour** shows real-life productions taking shape at the studio soundstages.

Disney Stars and Motor Cars Parade

A daily procession of amazing 'morphed' vehicles carrying the stars of your favourite Disney films.

Hollywood Boulevard and Sunset Boulevard

These two streets form the heart of the shopping and eating spots within the park. The far end of Sunset Boulevard has some of the best rides and shows. The huge skyscraper is **The Twilight Zone Tower of Terror™**, a ride through an abandoned and haunted hotel. Disney's first inverted ride, **Rock 'n' Roller Coaster® Starring Aerosmith**, takes you on a fantastic 3D ride through Disney's Los Angeles, with rock group Aerosmith providing the soundtrack. **Beauty and the Beast – Live on Stage** recreates the highlights of this hit Disney movie. **Walt Disney – One Man's Dream** is all about the man himself. It is great background knowledge for movie fans. There is a cavalcade of audio-animatronic stars at **The Great Movie Ride**, recreating some great MGM film moments, from Gene Kelly in *Singing in the Rain* to the monster from *Alien*. **Star Tours** highlights the realm of George Lucas films and features a spectacular space trip in a Star Speeder. In the **Indiana Jones™ Epic Stunt Spectacular!**, the explorer's greatest action sequences are replayed – with real-life actors taking all the risks. **Lights! Motors! Action!™** is an extreme stunt show including cars, motorcycles and watercraft. The **Sound Stage Experience** lets you look at the making of *The Chronicles of Narnia*.

Mickey Avenue

Mickey Avenue is home to a varied collection of attractions. The Disney's Hollywood™ Studios Backlot Tour, featuring **Catastrophe Canyon**, enters the world of special effects and tours parts of the studios that are normally off-limits to the public.

New York Street

At **Jim Henson's MuppetVision 3D** you dive into the chaos and hoopla of the Muppet Theater, where Kermit, Miss Piggy and Fozzie Bear really do look as though they are just in front of you, and the antics never stop.

TAKING A BREAK

The Sci-Fi Dine-In Theater Restaurant ££ A mock drive-in where you are served by waitresses on roller skates and you can watch non-stop black and white sci-fi film clips as you eat.

AFTER DARK

Fantasmic! Features Mickey Mouse in his role as the Sorcerer's Apprentice whose dreams take on a fantastic life of their own. It is entertainment on an epic scale, a true stage spectacular.

Best of the rest

In the last few years, Walt Disney World® Resort has grown far beyond Walt's own vision. Here are some highlights to choose from after you have enjoyed the main resort parks. Remember though that each of the following has its own admission charge and/or parking charges.

Disney's Blizzard Beach Water Park

Only Disney would consider creating a water-park themed on a ski resort, but Blizzard Beach is exactly that – a series of adventure 'zones' where the rides are all styled as ski, toboggan and bob-sleigh runs. Towering above is snow-capped Mount Gushmore – at 27.5 m (90 ft) it is the world's tallest free-fall flume. You can even take a chair-lift to the top for great views over the park.

ⓐ 1801 West Buena Vista Drive, Lake Buena Vista **ⓣ** 407 824 2222 or 1800 W DISNEY (freephone in US)

Disney's Typhoon Lagoon

One of the first Disney water-parks and the one many still consider the best, Typhoon Lagoon is themed on the aftermath of a tropical storm. Amongst the wooden shacks, flotsam and jetsam you will find a huge surf pool with perfect 1.5 m (5 ft) waves, surrounded by a wonderful fine sand beach and hammocks to laze the afternoon away. **Humunga Kowabunga** is a three-flume slide chute and there are body-slides, rafting courses and **Ketchakiddee** with activities especially for two- to six-year-olds. **Crush'n Gusher** is a new water coaster. You can also snorkel in a huge salt-water reef with rays, fish and real sharks (though not the ones that eat humans).

ⓐ Near Pleasure Island and the AMC Theater along Buena Vista Drive **ⓣ** 407 560 4141

Disney's Wide World of Sports® Complex

Disney's homage to the American love of sports is probably the least interesting attraction in the whole Walt Disney World® Resort to football-loving Brits. However, this complex is state-of-the-art, can cater to over 30 different sports and is beginning to attract some high-class sporting tournaments.

ⓐ Walt Disney World® Resort ☎ 407 824 2222 or 1800 W DISNEY (freephone in US) ⏰ Closed winter

Richard Petty Driving Experience

After all the roller coasters, water chutes and interactive games, the Richard Petty Driving Experience brings a thrilling touch of high-speed reality to Disney. Visitors here can enjoy the thrill of the 1.5 km (1 mile) oval racetrack in the capable hands of the professional drivers.

ⓐ Walt Disney World® Speedway at the Magic Kingdom® Park ☎ 407 939 0130 🅦 www.1800bepetty.com ❗ Reservations required

🔺 *Snow meets sun at Blizzard Beach* © Disney

Downtown Disney®

Although some of the Disney parks stay open late, the resort also has a purpose-built entertainment area that comes into its own at night. Downtown Disney® brings together restaurants, nightclubs, cinemas and live music venues, and hosts some of the most unusual shopping opportunities in Orlando. It is divided into three distinct areas: Downtown Disney® West Side, Pleasure Island and Marketplace.

THINGS TO SEE & DO

Cirque du Soleil®
A wonderful aerial spectacle, the Cirque du Soleil® show 'La Nouba' is a celebration of the acrobatic and gymnastic arts.
☎ 407 939 7600

DisneyQuest® Indoor Interactive Theme Park
A five-storey techno-park where you can try your hand at any number of virtual diversions, including cutting your own CD.

TAKING A BREAK

DOWNTOWN DISNEY® WEST SIDE
Bongos Cuban Café™ ££ Emilio and Gloria Estefan own this informal restaurant, which serves delicious Cuban food. As you would expect, the Latin music is great as well.

Planet Hollywood® ££ As always with this chain, some interesting memorabilia and a good range of food, from sandwiches to steaks.

PLEASURE ISLAND
Fulton's Crab House ££ A floating restaurant styled like an old river steamer. As you would expect, the menu leans heavily to seafood.

RESORT DETAILS
ⓐ Downtown Disney® I-4 exit 26B ☎ 407 WDW 2NITE (939 2648)
ⓦ www.downtowndisney.com
For all dining options at the resort ☎ 407 WDW-DINE (939 3463)

MARKET PLACE
Rainforest Café® ££ Wonderfully done, with an authentic rainforest soundtrack and audio-animatronic animals.

AFTER DARK

DOWNTOWN DISNEY® WEST SIDE
House of Blues® Based on the *Blues Brothers* film, this concert hall comes alive every night with a range of sounds from blues to rock to soul. There's even Gospel Brunch on Sundays.

🔺 *Meals and memorabilia at Planet Hollywood®* © Disney

AMC® PLEASURE ISLAND Pleasure Island has the main concentration of nightclub and live music venues in Downtown Disney®. There is a separate charge after dark and some age restrictions apply.

8TRAX Transports you back to the 1970s with non-stop hits from the era of bell-bottoms.

Adventurers' Club Watch the antics of a range of inventive cast members.

The BET Soundstage Club Showcases the latest in hip hop and R&B. Comedy Warehouse improvised stand-up routines come thick and fast.

Mannequin's Dance Palace With its revolving dance floor, this club has been voted the best dance venue in the US.

Motion Mainstream pop.

Pleasure Island Jazz Company Try this club for a little syncopation.

Raglan Road This is a popular Irish pub.

Rock 'n Roll Beach Club Rock classics.

MARKETPLACE
Marketplace is the main shopping section of Downtown Disney®, with a range of individual and interesting stores.
Art of Disney If you are into cartoon memorabilia, including original cartoon 'cells', then this is the shop for you.
Lego Imagination Center® This interactive playground and shop will keep children happy for hours; Lego kits for sale too.
World of Disney® The anchor store of Marketplace, this is also the largest Disney store in the world.

Universal Orlando® Resort

Universal Orlando® Resort is situated just off International Drive and I-4 and encompasses two huge theme parks, Universal Studios Florida® and Islands of Adventure®. A 12.5 ha (30 acre) entertainment park, CityWalk, doubles as a gateway to both theme parks.

Orlando was the natural location for Universal to build a theme park based on their blockbuster hit films. Disney's roller coasters and 3D rides just don't stack up against the Universal experience – Universal Studios Florida®, which opened in 1990, was an immediate success, with the best rides, in this ride-packed town. In 1999 Universal opened Islands of Adventure®, considered the most complete theme park experience in the world. Who could fail to be impressed with Steven Spielberg as creative consultant? Also opened in 1999, and linking the two, CityWalk provides a huge variety of restaurants, themed restaurants, nightclubs, state-of-the-art cinemas and live entertainment venues.

◆ *All aboard for the best rides in town*

Universal Studios Florida®

While the Universal Studios Florida® theme park appeals more to older children and adults than to young kids, the park attempts to entertain young ones with a special section just for them. The park is divided into themed areas surrounding an artificial lake where you can take boat rides or enjoy a meal at one of a range of restaurants.

THINGS TO SEE & DO

HOLLYWOOD
Lucy: A Tribute^{SM}
Fantastic fun for fans of the *I Love Lucy* TV series, with classic shows, scripts and costumes.

Terminator 2®: 3D Battle Across Time
Based on the hugely successful Hollywood blockbuster, this 'part show, part film' puts you in the heart of the action. A Cyberdyne Systems demonstration is hijacked and you travel into the future to watch John and his Terminator protector attempt to save the world. The original cast and director filmed 12 minutes of extra footage purely for this attraction, and it cost more to shoot than the original *Terminator 2* film, but was definitely worth it. The 3D effects are spectacular and it's well worth seeing.

Universal Horror Make-Up Show
Teenagers and adults will be fascinated by this film which shows just how actors are turned into scary monsters or mutilated victims.

NEW YORK
The Blues Brothers®
Jake and Elwood Blues (well, not the real guys) get together daily to perform a selection of hits from their film. It is great entertainment, but even better if you have seen the film and can sing along.

Revenge of the Mummy℠: The Ride
Battle flesh-eating scarab beetles and face an army of mummy warriors. Will you survive?

Twister – Ride It Out®
Based on the hit film, this attraction recreates a little of what it feels like to encounter a tornado – obviously it is not as bad as the real thing!

PRODUCTION CENTRAL
Just beyond the entrance to the park, Production Central has all the guest service facilities. This is where you sign up to be in the audience of any TV productions that are taking place that day.

Jimmy Neutron's Nicktoon Blast™
Jimmy's friend Carl and his robot dog, Goddard, invite everyone to help Jimmy recover his stolen rocket and save the planet from scoundrel villain Ooblar. On the way, *The Fairly OddParents*, *The Rugrats* and *SpongeBob SquarePants* add more fun to this frantic simulator ride.

Nickelodeon Studios
Nickelodeon is the number-one American TV network for kids and it is here that the programmes are made. Definitely one for the under-tens.

Shrek 4-D™
Mindblowing digital show with surprising and innovative sensory elements. OgreVision glasses and specially designed seats make everyone part of the new adventures of Shrek, Fiona and Donkey. One of the best new shows in Orlando.

SAN FRANCISCO/AMITY
Beetlejuice's Graveyard Revue™
A musical spectacular bringing together a gruesome collection of performers from Frankenstein to the Wolfman.

◔ *Just when you thought it was safe ...*

Disaster℠
Initially, the attraction spends time explaining how the special effects for the film were achieved, before you get to find out just what it feels like to live through an earthquake. As you travel through the San Francisco subway, the earthquake begins. Then the tunnel collapses, fires explode around you and you begin to get a sense of the terror involved.

Jaws®
Just when you thought it was safe to go back on another ride you reach Amity, and your quiet boat trip becomes a fight for survival as the 10 m (32 ft) shark wants you for his next meal.

WOODY WOODPECKER'S KIDZONE®
If some of the rides at Universal prove too scary for small children, Woody Woodpecker's Kidzone® is a place where they are sure to feel at home. There is plenty to enjoy, and a few familiar characters to meet along the way, including Woody himself, Barney the dinosaur and ET.

Animal Actors On Location℠
A number of rescue animals and old animal film stars from Universal pictures appear on stage, showing off a range of stunts and helped by a few small members of the audience.

Curious George Goes To Town℠
An action-packed playground that includes water games.

A Day In The Park With Barney™
The only place on earth where kids can meet this friendly purple dinosaur, and he hosts his own stage show with lots of sing-along children's songs.

ET Adventure®
Head out over the imaginary treetops at ET Adventure® where you follow everyone's favourite alien on your flying bikes. A pleasant journey with glorious scenery, though thrill seekers may find it a little tame.

Fievel's Playground®

The cartoon mouse invites children to get physical with themed climbing frames, slides and trampolines.

Woody Woodpecker's Nuthouse Coaster®

This is the answer to those frustrating height restrictions on the larger rides. Anyone over 1 m (3 ft) can ride, and though it goes slowly compared with adult rides, it divides kids into two camps – those who want to ride over and over, and those who will never try a roller coaster again.

WORLD EXPO
Men in Black™ – Alien Attack™

Do you want to save the Earth from aliens? As a trainee agent you head off on the adventure of a lifetime, zapping monsters with your ray gun. Unfortunately the aliens shoot back and you need to get a better score than them in order to save the earth. It is like being in the middle of a huge computer game and the plot changes, depending on how skilled you are, so you may not have the same ride twice.

TAKING A BREAK

Mel's Drive-In £ Burgers, hot dogs and milk shakes in this 1950s-style diner themed on the one in the film *American Graffiti* starring Richard Dreyfuss. ❸ At Hollywood

Finnegan's Bar and Grill ££ Familiar dishes include shepherd's pie and corn-beef hash in this New York-style eatery, with more than a leaning towards the Emerald Isle. ❸ At New York

Lombard's Seafood Grille ££ Overlooking the inner lagoon, Lombard's Landing is the largest eatery at Universal Studios and offers a choice of seafood, salads and sandwiches. ❸ At San Francisco/Amity

Islands of Adventure®

Universal's second theme park, Islands of Adventure®, is next to Universal Studios Florida® and is rated as the most complete theme park in Orlando, which is saying something when you look at the competition. There are attractions for all members of the family here and more thrilling five-star rides than in any other park, for those who need that adrenalin rush! The park is divided into five themed islands, connected by bridges circled around the lake, and the Port of Entry with its shops and restaurants.

THINGS TO SEE & DO

JURASSIC PARK®
Step into the world of *Jurassic Park*, the film, to find many different experiences, all with a prehistoric theme.

Camp Jurassic®
A perfect playground for mini-dinosaur hunters, including an 'active' volcano to explore.

Jurassic Park Discovery Center®
Watch a baby dinosaur hatch, or mix your DNA with a dinosaur in a computer simulation – just two of the interactive exhibits here.

Jurassic Park River Adventure®
The theme for this ride is a river journey through the landscape of the Cretaceous period. You catch glimpses of raptors in the undergrowth – but where is the T-Rex? Be ready to make a dramatic escape!

Pteranodon Flyers®
Youngsters can fly over Jurassic Park, carried by giant pteranodons. Riders must be 1–1.5 m (3–4 ft 8 in) tall or be accompanied by a height-qualified rider.

THE LOST CONTINENT®

If many Jurassic Park® attractions have a pseudo-scientific feel, The Lost Continent® is pure fantasy. Universal's twist on Atlantis, the World of 1001 Knights and a host of other legendary lands.

Dueling Dragons®

A roller coaster with a difference. There are two inverted roller coasters and through a series of twists, loops and one 30.5 m (100 ft) drop, you come hair-raisingly close to collision with the other group of riders – at speeds of nearly 90 km/h (55 mph).

The Eighth Voyage of Sinbad

Follow the adventures of Sinbad and his sidekick as they rescue Princess Amoura from the clutches of evil witch Miseria. This live show has some good special effects and the cast pull off some energetic stunts.

The Flying Unicorn®

A junior-sized roller coaster ride for six- to twelve-year-olds.

Poseidon's Fury®

Enter Poseidon's underwater realm in this walk-through multimedia attraction. Features a fantastic final duel scene between Zeus, armed with fire, and Poseidon, armed with water.

MARVEL SUPER HERO ISLAND®

This is where the heroes step out of the pages of Marvel Comics to meet and greet – lots of opportunities for photo sessions.

The Amazing Adventures of Spider-Man®

An audio-visual spectacular puts you in the heart of the battle between Spider-Man®, alias ace reporter Peter Parker, and his arch-enemies. With the 3D effects and the motion simulator, you will feel every move that 'Spidey' makes, including a drop off a skyscraper that leaves your stomach in your mouth.

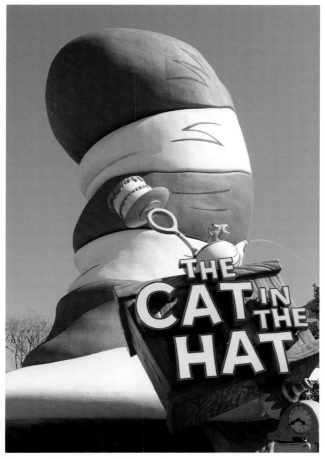

● *A spectacular Seuss-based ride*

Doctor Doom's Fearfall®

One minute you are sitting on the ground, the next you are heading skyward at breakneck speed to the top of the 61 m (200 ft) tower with a view over much of Orlando. A quick ride, but very exhilarating.

Incredible Hulk Coaster®

If it's a Hulk Coaster®, then it's got to be big and dramatic. This roller coaster heads out over Islands of Adventure® lagoon at speeds of up to 105 km/h (65 mph), turning you every which way.

Storm Force Accelatron®

This milder fairground-style ride, with special effects, is particularly suited to young visitors.

SEUSS LANDING™

Enter the kooky world of Dr Seuss, where everything rhymes and there are no straight lines. Most kids will know *The Grinch* cartoon film and he is just one of many characters here. A magnet for the under-fives.

Caro-Seuss-el™

An old-fashioned carousel ride with Seuss characters instead of horses.

The Cat In The Hat™

Ride through the story of *The Cat in the Hat*™. Your coaster takes you up and around the slinky Seuss animals.

If I Ran The Zoo™

An interactive play park with lots of activities, most of which seem to include getting wet.

One Fish, Two Fish, Red Fish, Blue Fish™

This fairground-style ride is a great hit with young riders. You must make the Seuss-style fish travel up and down in time with the music. If you fail, you get fired on from mini-water cannons.

TOON LAGOON®

Enter the world of comic hero Popeye for a series of 'watery' experiences.

Dudley Do-Right's Ripsaw Falls®

Another option for a soaking, this time an 18 m (60 ft) drop is part of the action.

🔺 *Seuss Landing™ – great for younger children*

Me Ship, The Olive^{SM}

Popeye's boat is full of interactive games for small kids. Best of all you can fire water at the people passing on Bilge-Rat Barges®.

Popeye and Bluto's Bilge-Rat Barges®

If Popeye organises a boat trip you just know that you are going to get very wet. It is not just the waves and waterfalls: you will be attacked from the banks by water cannon.

TAKING A BREAK

Green Eggs and Ham™ Café £ Try the meal of the same name, invented by Dr Seuss himself – and yes the eggs are green!
🅐 At Seuss Landing™

Mythos Restaurant® ££ Styled as the inside of a dormant volcano, you eat amongst underground waterfalls and lava plumes. Serves good-quality steak, chicken, pizza and seafood. 🅐 At The Lost Continent®

UNIVERSAL ORLANDO RESORT® DETAILS
🅐 1000 Universal Boulevard 📞 407 363 8000
🌐 www.universalorlando.com 🕐 09.00–18.00 daily (later in summer; CityWalk 11.00–23.00) ❗ Admission charge

Universal CityWalk®

Universal's latest attraction takes the excitement into the evening hours. This entertainment village combines shopping, dining, live performances and the latest silver screen epics. Though it is open during the day (it links the two Universal theme parks and is a popular place for lunch and snacks), the atmosphere of Universal CityWalk® is more highly charged after nightfall. Age restrictions apply to enter nightclubs.

TAKING A BREAK

Restaurants & bars
Nascar® Sports Grille £ Themed on the Nascar racing formula, there are real cars outside for you to admire and races on TV inside. Menu includes burgers, chicken and ribs. 🕒 11.00–late daily

Hard Rock Café® ££ The world's largest Hard Rock Café®, with interesting memorabilia and great music. 🕒 11.00–late daily

Jimmy Buffet's® Margaritaville® ££ The musician and native Floridian Jimmy Buffet owns this bar/diner. Laidback island style is the influence, with lots of seafood, salads and pasta on the menu. Live music or Jimmy's own. 🕒 11.00–late daily

Pastamoré℠ Ristoranté & Market ££ This is a casual, family-style Italian restaurant and an outdoor market place café. 🅰 1000 Universal Studios Plaza ☎ 407 224 4663 🕒 17.00–24.00 daily, café 08.00–02.00

Emeril's® Restaurant Orlando £££ Famed New Orleans chef Emeril Lagasse brings his Cajun-influenced menu and impeccable Continental-style service to Universal. This is one place to really push the boat out. ☎ 407 224 2424 🕒 11.30–14.00, 17.30–22.00 Sun–Thur, 11.30–14.00, 17.30–23.00 Fri & Sat ❗ Reservations recommended

Orlando Palm® £££ The same family have owned the upmarket Palm® restaurants chain since 1926 and this eatery, the latest in the stable, is already a hit with Orlando natives as well as with visitors. Signature dishes are excellent steaks and chops, although you can also choose from a range of seafood dishes. Excellent wine list. ⓐ 5800 Universal Boulevard at the Hard Rock Hotel® ⓣ 407 503 7256 ⓛ 17.00–late daily ⓘ Reservations recommended

AFTER DARK

Bob Marley: A Tribute to Freedom℠ The recreation of Bob Marley's Jamaican home is the setting for great live reggae music and the restaurant serves jerk pork and chicken. ⓛ 14.00–02.00 daily

CityJazz® Combines a tribute to the great jazz icons with a venue for the latest in live jazz. Tapas bar. ⓛ 20.00–02.00 daily

the groove℠ Disco/club with the latest dance music, 70s night, 80s disco and teen night on Fridays. ⓛ 21.00–02.00 daily

Hard Rock Live® Concert venue for mid- to big-name musicians; see the schedule at ⓦ www.hardrocklive.com

Latin Quarter™ The latest Latin sounds with guest DJs or live bands, along with great spicy South American food. ⓛ 17.00–02.00 Mon–Fri, 12.00–02.00 Sat & Sun

SeaWorld®

One of the world's leading aquatic theme parks, SeaWorld® is both an entertainment centre and education facility, offering exciting animal shows, attention-grabbing exhibits and the chance to find out more about how you can help to save the world's oceans. The team behind SeaWorld® and Busch Gardens® are also launching Aquatica®, Florida's first major theme park in 15 years. See ⓦ www.AquaticabySeaworld.com for details.

If you want VIP treatment at SeaWorld®, book the Adventure Express Tour (extra charge). You will have a personal guide, priority access to rides, seats at the shows and opportunities to feed the animals.

THINGS TO SEE & DO

Blue Horizons
Dolphins, false killer whales and exotic birds including blue and gold macaws, sun conures and an Andean condor cavort above and below the water.

Clyde and Seamore Take Pirate Island
A hilarious show featuring playful sea lions and a cheeky otter. The pre-show mime is well worth seeing at the Sea Lion and Otter Stadium. After the show see a whole collection of sea lions and walruses with their own wave machine recreating their natural breakwater environment.

THEME PARK DETAILS
🅐 7007 SeaWorld Drive, off International Drive ☏ 407 363 2613 or 800 327 2424 (freephone in US) ⓦ www.seaworld.com
🕐 09.00–19.00 (later in summer)

⬥ *The manatee pool at SeaWorld®*

Journey to Atlantis

SeaWorld®'s water-coaster ride takes you on a voyage to a lost world, with many damp adventures enroute, and one dramatic drenching. The special effects and audio-visuals are extremely impressive.

Key West at SeaWorld®

The dolphins play in their vast sea water pool – Dolphin Cove. There are several feeding times during the day when the dolphins will come and take fish from your hand. The Key West Dolphin Fest show takes place at the nearby stadium. Key West also has Turtle Point and Stingray Lagoon, where you can hand-feed these unusual flat fish.

Kraken

Kraken is the longest, fastest and highest ride in Orlando. You dangle (safely of course) from a 'floorless mega-coaster' and so the ride feels even more thrilling.

Manatee Rescue

Manatees, also known as sea cows, are gentle slow-moving creatures that graze on vegetation in the coastal shallows and inter-coastal waterways. You can watch these endangered mammals from above and below the water, and learn about programmes to protect them in the wild.

Odyssea

A unique 30-minute underwater-themed circus and acrobatics exhibition.

Penguin Encounter

Penguins 'do their thing', totally oblivious to the audience on the other side of the viewing screen. Look out for the baby penguins – they look just like the fluffy bearskin busbies worn by the guards outside Buckingham Palace.

Pets Ahoy

A funny show featuring a variety of small animals, from dogs to pot-bellied pigs, most of them from rescue homes. At the SeaWorld® Theater.

Shamu Stadium

Although SeaWorld® is now far more than the killer whale show that originally made it famous, Shamu and his relatives are still probably the most popular attractions in the park. These huge mammals perform graceful manoeuvres in the large display pool, but everyone really comes for the finale when their huge tails splash water out into the

ACTIVITIES

SeaWorld® runs several interactive programmes including an **Animal Care Experience, False Killer Whale Interaction Program**, and a **Trainer for a Day Program** (extra charge). These need to be booked well in advance. ☎ 407 370 1382 or 800 327 2424 (freephone in US) 🌐 www.seaworld.com

auditorium, soaking everyone in the lower seats. Kids just love it! Parents – protect your cameras from the salt water.

Sky Tower

You get a fantastic panorama of greater Orlando plus great sunsets from this 120 m (400 ft) viewing platform (extra charge).

Wild Arctic

Take a simulated helicopter ride over this frozen landscape to the 'research station' at Base Arctic Wild. Here you will see the inhospitable environment that the polar bear, walruses and beluga whales call home.

TAKING A BREAK

Mango Joe's Café £ A delicious range of sandwiches, including hot offerings of beef, chicken and fish, also Mexican fajitas, salads and numerous side items. ❷ Near Shamu Stadium and Wild Arctic

🔻 *Get soaked by Shamu at SeaWorld®*

Discovery Cove®

Discovery Cove®, a sister attraction to SeaWorld®, recreates a desert island hideaway. Here, you can spend a day away from the crowds and hi-tech theme parks and relax on soft white beaches or swim in teeming waters. Not only that, but there is the opportunity to swim with a dolphin – you cannot do that anywhere else in Orlando.

Discovery Cove® aims to offer an exclusive experience, which means that the 12 ha (30 acres) of lush landscaped park is open to just 1000 people each day. It is the most expensive adventure park in the city and reservations in advance are required, but you are guaranteed few queues, lots of space and a very personal service. Think of it as a five-star resort without the hotel room and you'll get the right idea. There is a high staff-to-guest ratio and the staff make plenty of time to answer all your questions.

You will be given towels, snorkel, goggles and flippers to use. There are wet suits in case you find the 26°C (80°F) water cold (you need to

⏏ *Swim like a ray*

THEME PARK DETAILS
ⓐ Entrance next to the Central Florida Parkway ☏ 877 434 7268
ⓦ www.discoverycove.com

wear this or a Discovery Cove® life jacket while in the water for safety
purposes) and there are buoyancy aids for poor swimmers. A decent
lunch is also included in the price (other snacks are reasonably priced).
The park has been divided into a number of different environments.

Admission to Discovery Cove® also provides seven days' unlimited
access to SeaWorld®. See website for details.

THINGS TO SEE & DO

Aviary
Part of the tropical river section leads into the aviary, and you can also
reach it on foot along the beach. There is an interesting and varied
collection of tropical birds, including peacocks, which are housed
amongst trees within a high net boundary that lets in lots of light
and fresh air. At feeding time the cheeky ones fly to your hand for
a snack.

Coral Reef
Filled with thousands of tropical fish and monster-sized rays lounging on
the bottom, this huge pool recreates a coral marine environment. Swim
around the remains of a wooden boat 'shipwrecked' here. Although the
coral is not real you will be amazed at the sheer numbers of jack fish and
angelfish – they swarm around you at feeding time (some young children
may find this a little disconcerting). The predators are at one end of the
reef, separated from the fish and human visitors by a sheet of strong
Plexiglas®. Look through it to see the sharks and barracuda swimming
around on the look-out for their next meal.

◆ *Get up close and personal during the Dolphin Swim*

The Dolphin Swim

Undoubtedly the highlight of your day at Discovery Cove®, the dolphin encounter allows you to get up close and personal with one of the most intelligent and thought-provoking creatures on the planet. When you book in at Discovery Cove® you will be given a time for your Dolphin Swim (extra charge). You receive a 15-minute introductory session before you enter the dolphin lagoon and, once in the water, one of the very professional animal trainers, who make both the humans and the dolphins feel at ease, will guide you. Group sizes range from six to twelve but everyone gets to have their photograph taken and play with one of these delightful mammals. It's a good idea to wear a wet suit for your encounter, as the water is colder than you think and you will spend well over 15 minutes being fairly inactive while you wait your turn.

Ray Lagoon

Next door to the coral reef, this lagoon is full of small- to medium-sized rays. You can attempt to emulate their graceful movement through the water.

Tropical River Swim

Swim or snorkel along an 800 m (875 yard) recreation of a tropical river (the water running through here is much warmer than the pools but has no sea life). You will encounter tropical forests along the banks, underwater ruins to explore and the opportunity to swim through a waterfall into the aviary.

If you don't want to take part in any of the swimming activities, or you simply want to rest in the sunshine, you can take your place on one of the numerous sun-beds on the soft white sand and pretend you are at the beach. Relax, and you will think you are a thousand miles away.

▶ *Sunset over the Florida coast*

EXCURSIONS
Out & about

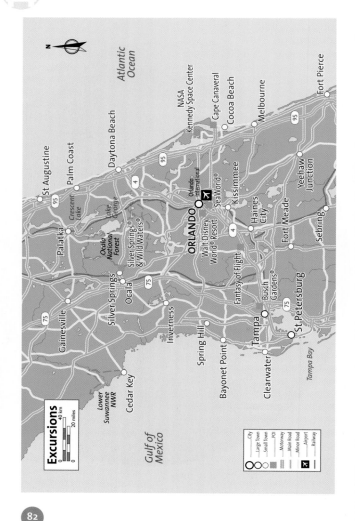

Busch Gardens®

Advertised as 'a wild world', Busch Gardens® is to the land what SeaWorld® is to the oceans. However, this park is not only a place to see animals from all over the world, it is also a place to enjoy the most exhilarating coasters in Florida. The combination of zoo, wildlife park and fairground makes it one of the most entertaining places to take a family. It is divided into a number of separate areas, themed on exotic African locations.

THINGS TO SEE & DO

Bird Gardens
The quietest part of the park, with bird exhibits and shows.

Congo
A great area for exhilarating rides. **Kumba**, one of the largest roller coasters in the southern USA, reaches 95 km/h (60 mph) and has a loop that plummets 33.5 m (110 ft) and a 360° spiral that leaves you weightless. **Python** whips along like a fast-moving snake and reaches 80 km/h (50 mph). **Congo River Rapids** carries your rubber raft over some realistic white water – be warned, you will get drenched. **Claw Island**, the tiger enclosure, sits in a gorge surrounded by a lagoon. You can look down on the animals lazing or playing in the water below. On **Skyride** you can glide serenely across the park in a four-person aerial gondola, with a view over the Rhino Rally ride. **Lory Landing** is chock-a-block with colourful parrots, hornbills and pheasants flying free within an enormous, domed aviary.

Edge of Africa
A walk-through tour of a section of the Serengeti Plain, where Plexiglas® screens are all that keep you and the animals apart. You will find a range of African species here including meerkats, vultures, hyenas, lions, crocodiles and baboons, not to mention hippos that you can view from

above and below the water. **The KaTonga Musical** is a lavishly produced 35-minute musical featuring African folklore set to song and dance.

Egypt

Montu, one of the largest inverted roller coasters in the world, reaches a G-force of 3.85, with speeds up to 95 km/h (60 mph) that see you hopping under and over the Busch Gardens® railway and high above the plains. Three minutes of total exhilaration. **Tut's Tomb** is a recreation of the treasure rooms found by Howard Carter in the Valley of the Kings in 1922.

The Land Of The Dragons

A lovely area geared to younger children under 142 cm (56 inches), with a three-storey tree-house, dragons strolling the paths and a selection of children's shows.

Gwazi

This dual roller coaster has one lion-coaster and one tiger-coaster that pass within feet of each other six times over the course of the 2,134 m (7,000 ft) long ride. It recreates the feel of a classic wooden roller coaster as it shakes you around in your seat.

Morocco

The entrance area is styled on an Oriental kasbah. Marrakesh Theater hosts **Moroccan Roll**, featuring pop songs with a northern African theme. Watch out for the **Mystic Sheiks of Morocco**, an all brass marching band which inspires dance parties through the streets.

Nairobi

Some heavyweight animal exhibits including elephants, gorillas and chimps. The primates' home is a specially created African central highland environment, one of the largest outside the continent.

● *See the wildlife on a jeep safari with a few surprises on the way!*

Rhino Rally

This is probably the best single ride in northern Florida for its clever combination of wildlife spotting, well-executed watery surprises and the attention to detail in the landscaping. Rhino Rally takes you on a Jeep safari through rhino country (real rhinos too!), where the animals wander in their park enclosure. Of course, your rally will not go totally to plan – that is the most exciting part! Try to do this ride early or late in the day because the animals seek shade in the heat of the afternoon.

THEME PARK DETAILS

ⓐ Busch Blvd, Tampa ⓣ General information 813 987 5082 or 888 800 5447 (freephone in US); Orlando recorded info 407 351 3931 ⓦ www.buschgardens.com ⓛ High season 10.00–18.00 Mon–Fri, 09.00–21.00 Sat & Sun ⓘ Admission charge

Serengeti Plain

Similar to Disney's Animal Kingdom® Park, the animals (gazelles, giraffe, zebra, rhino and buffalo) roam freely across the 20 ha (50 acre) recreation of an African savannah. The Busch Gardens® railway carries you sedately around the area, giving you plenty of time to view the

🔺 *Congo River Rapids at Busch Gardens®*

animals. Alternatively, book your own safari experience, where you head into the Serengeti Plain in a truck, at Edge of Africa (extra charge).

Stanleyville

ShiekRa, Busch Gardens®' newest roller coaster, is Florida's tallest, and billed as North America's first 'dive coaster'. It's a three-minute, 113 km/h (70 mph) rocket-ride up 61 m (200 ft), then 90° straight down, through an Immelman loop (try to scratch your nose!), then a *second* 90° drop... down through a tunnel... and more! **Tanganyika Tidal Wave** takes you through the uncharted waterways of Africa before plummeting over the edge of undiscovered waterfalls. **Stanley Falls** is a roller coaster-style log flume ride. The major animal exhibit of Stanleyville is **Orang-utans**. **Stanleyville Theater** is home to the 'Jungle Fantasy' stage show featuring acrobatics and circus-style acts.

Timbuktu

Timbuktu features a range of old-fashioned fairground arcade games and smaller fairground rides for kids. The **Scorpion** roller coaster will provide you with a 360° loop and two minutes of heart-stopping fun.

TAKING A BREAK

Zagora Café **££** There is a large outdoor eating area where you will be serenaded by a Louisiana-style marching brass band.

> ### SHUTTLE BUS
> The Busch Gardens® Shuttle Express departs Orlando daily from the Universal bus park at 08.30, SeaWorld® bus parking at 08.45, Old Town Shopping Village Kissimmee at 09.15 (except Sat) and Orlando Premium Outlets at 09.30. Tickets are $10 round trip per person at the time of writing or free with a flex-ticket. For reservations (required) call ☎ 800 221 1339 (freephone in US).

◓ *Plenty of space to catch some rays at Cocoa Beach*

Beach resorts

CLEARWATER

Head west of Tampa after your visit to Busch Gardens® and you will hit the west coast of Florida, which is bounded by the Gulf of Mexico that eventually stretches around to Texas and into Mexico itself. Although there are excellent beaches all along the 'Gulf Coast', as it is known here, **Clearwater** has extra acres of soft white sand and has captured the market as far as hotels and restaurants are concerned. There are no major attractions in the area but the atmosphere is very family-oriented, the perfect antidote if you have had too much of Orlando.

COCOA BEACH

The closest beach resort to Orlando is **Cocoa Beach** – a laid back family resort with a long, wide beach and a rustic wooden pier. You can buy bait for fishing or simply sit and have an *al fresco* lunch, walk for miles along the shore or play volleyball. It is a good place to chill out. One thing that most locals head to Cocoa for is the surfing (though by world standards the waves are not great) and it is the cool place for American college students at spring break.

DAYTONA BEACH

Yet another Florida beach resort, but this is one with a difference. Since the early 1920s, Daytona's name has been synonymous with motor

SHOPPING

Even if you do not surf, visit **Ron Jon's Surf Shop**, a Florida institution visited by more than 2.4 million people annually. You will be able to buy just about any surf gear, swimwear or tropical clothing here. It is hard to miss this huge pink castle-like building on the main road. ❷ 4151 North Atlantic Avenue, Cocoa Beach ❶ 321 799 8888 ❿ www.ronjons.com ❶ 24 hours daily

racing. In the early days, lots of speed records were broken here but eventually it was deemed too dangerous to race on the wide, flat, hard-packed sandy beach, though a legacy of that time is that motor vehicles are still allowed out on the sand. Cruising along the beach here at a stately 8 km/h (5 mph) is one of the classic must-do American activities.

Speed fans can still get a thrill at the **Daytona Race Circuit** opened in 1959, where both bike and car formulas meet throughout the year (For dates and ticket details ☎ 904 253 7223). Next door to the circuit is **Daytona USA**, where you can test your skills at changing a wheel in a pit stop, take a guided tour of the track or try three laps in the hands of a professional driver (ⓐ 1801 W. International Speed Blvd ☎ 386 947 6800 ⓦ www.daytonausa.com). **The Richard Petty Driving Experience** also offers an extensive range of driving experiences (☎ 800 237 3889 ⓦ www.1800bepetty.com ⓛ 09.00–19.00 daily except Christmas)

🔺 *Join the cool dudes on Daytona Beach*

Fantasy of Flight

The largest private collection of rare and vintage aircraft in the world, Fantasy of Flight is the personal dream come true of multi-millionaire Kermit Weeks and it is still expanding. It's a fascinating place to explore, especially for lovers of aircraft.

Whet your appetite with the film **History of Flight** before heading for the **Vintage Aircraft** hangars with over 40 specimens, including the Spitfire of World War II fame. At **Fightertown** you can try your hand in a World War II fighter simulator to take on the enemy in aerial combat. Aviation buffs should take one of the guided tours, and bi-plane, warbird and balloon rides are highly recommended.

ⓐ 1400 Broadway Boulevard, Polk City ❶ 863 984 3500
ⓦ www.fantasyofflight.com ❷ 09.00–17.00 daily ❶ Admission charge

⬤ *Be amazed at the world's largest collection of vintage planes*

NASA Kennedy Space Center

When the space race reached its climax in the late 1960s, the eyes of the whole world were on the Kennedy Space Center on the east coast of Florida, about 45 minutes from Orlando. This was the nerve centre of operations, a place where the then state-of-the-art technology allowed humans to land on the Moon and to return safely back to Earth. Now it is home to the Space Shuttle programme and one of the Earth's two working spaceports – and the only one open to the public. There is really nothing quite as thrilling as watching a shuttle rising from its launch pad. If there is a launch during your stay, try not to miss it.

THINGS TO SEE & DO

A visit has two main components: exhibits at the Visitor Complex and the Kennedy Space Center coach tour. If you arrive at the Space Center around late morning, take the tour first before it gets crowded.

VISITOR COMPLEX
Your visit will start at the Visitor Complex, the exhibition area for the Kennedy complex which has a range of exhibits and activities.

Astronaut Encounter
Chat to a real astronaut and find out what food tastes like in space.

Early Space Exploration
This exhibit takes you back to the build-up to orbit. Pride of place is taken by a reconstruction of the control centre for the early Mercury space launches and it is amazing to think that today's home PC has more computing power than they had at their fingertips.

Exploration in the New Millennium
Lots of fun hands-on scientific stuff for children. The highlight is being able to touch a piece of rock that was brought back from Mars.

◆ *Blasting off at Cape Canaveral*

CENTER DETAILS

a On the SR 405 east (NASA Parkway) **☏** 321 449 4444
w www.kennedyspacecenter.com **⏱** 09.00–17.30 or later
(daily, except Christmas and launch days) **ⓘ** Admission charge

Mad Mission to Mars Show

This is the kind of science class that you wanted at school, with lots of
kooky experiments and audience participation.

Robot Scouts

A display explaining the role of unmanned space flights such as probes
bringing back information from the surrounding planets.

Rocket Garden

Your chance to get close to some of the old rockets that provided the
thrust to break out of the Earth's atmosphere.

Shuttle Plaza

Look inside a full-sized replica of the Space Shuttle to see how little room
the astronauts live in while on their missions. Head across the square to
Launch Status Center to hear flight briefings every hour and get an
overview of the launch programme.

THE SPACE CENTER COACH TOUR

The visitor complex exhibits are excellent, but they should be taken as a
whole with the coach tour, which takes you behind the scenes into the
real working part of the Space Center. The bus makes three stops, but
there's a lot to observe as you travel between them.

Apollo/Saturn V Center

This stop brings the space race and the first landing on the Moon back to
life. You can examine a full-scale recreation of the Apollo control centre and
relive the tension by watching actual footage of the missions.

The LC-39 Observation Gantry

From the top of LC-39 you'll get some of the best panoramic views in Florida. You'll easily spot the huge Space Shuttle launch pads and the Vehicle Assembly Building (VAB) whose interior is so large it has rained inside. There is also a theatre presentation and interactive exhibit room.

US Astronaut Hall of Fame®

This fascinating attraction has personal insights from the astronauts themselves, highlighting their role from the first manned missions through to the Space Shuttle and Space Station programmes. Kids will enjoy the interactive elements in **Astronaut Adventure** with its G-Force machines and flight simulators.

ⓐ On the SR 405 east (NASA Parkway) ❶ 321 269 6100

ⓦ www.astronauthalloffame.com 🕒 10.00–18.30 daily

❶ Admission charge

SHUTTLE LAUNCHES

To find out if there are any launches scheduled during your holiday, contact Kennedy Space Center (❶ 321 449 4400) or look on the website (ⓦ www.kennedyspacecenter.com). For free tickets to the special viewing area, phone (❶ 321 449 4400) or apply online (ⓦ www.ksctickets.com/kennedyspacecenter). You may also write at least three months in advance (ⓐ NASA Visitor Services, Mail Code: PA-PASS, Kennedy Space Center Visitor Center, FL 32899). If you are not lucky enough to get a ticket, stake out a spot along Highway 1 or A1A (especially the inter-coastal sections), where you can still get a great view. As a last resort, you can see the shuttle from much of the state soon after blast-off: just look up.

Silver Springs®

Based around one of the largest freshwater springs in the world, Silver Springs® is a beautiful 142 ha (350 acre) park.

THINGS TO SEE & DO

Big Gator Lagoon
This attraction really lives up to its name, with lots of huge denizens lying in 0.4 ha (1 acre) of genuine cypress swampland – their natural habitat.

Birds of Prey
A show that highlights the tremendous strength, flexibility and accuracy of the large bird species.

Botanical Gardens
Do take time to stroll through the botanical gardens, with more than 130 varieties of native and exotic plants, floral sculptures and flowerbeds.

Crocodile Encounter
Crocs from around the world are here, from the Australian 'salty' to the rapier-snouted fish-eating gharial. 🕐 Feeding 14.30 daily in summer

Florida Natives
A collection of animals still found in the backwoods of the state, including several species of snakes, otters and turtles.

Fort King River Cruise
Visit an actual archaeological dig site, a reconstructed Seminole Indian village and a 19th-century Fort King Army stockade.

Glass-bottomed boat trips
Discover a wealth of wildlife including turtles, huge freshwater fish, herons, egrets, waterfowl and the occasional baby 'gator.

🔺 *Glass-bottomed boat, Silver Springs®*

Kritter Korral
This is a petting zoo for the little ones, with soft, friendly farm animals

Lost River Voyage
Explore an untamed stretch of the river and its dense forest canopy for native wildlife spotting. Includes a trip to the park's veterinary hospital.

Panther Prowl
This attraction breeds panthers in captivity and educates visitors about this beautiful species which is in danger of extinction.

Ross Allen Island Animal Shows
Three different shows featuring reptiles, birds and creepy-crawlies.

World of Bears
The largest captive bear collection in the world.

THEME PARK DETAILS
🚌 East of Ocala on the SR40 (exit 352 east off I-75 or exit 268 west off I-95) ☎ 352 236 2121 🌐 www.silversprings.com
🕐 Open year round 10.00–17.00 daily ❶ Admission charge

St Augustine

St Augustine is the oldest continuously occupied settlement in the United States. In 1565, Spanish forces under Pedro Menéndez de Avilés founded the town, which then changed nationality several times between the Spanish and the English before American independence. Many of St Augustine's historic buildings still remain, and the old downtown area recreates life in those early days so you can really get a feel for the founding of this new country.

THINGS TO SEE & DO

Castillo de San Marcos

Built by the Spanish, the fort town was finished in 1697 and is one of only a handful in North America. You can walk around the battlements and take in the panoramic views. During the summer, battles are re-enacted on the pristine lawns within the castle grounds – it is thrilling stuff with the clash of iron and the smell of gunpowder.
ⓐ 1 Castillo Drive, off Avenida Menéndez ⓣ 904 829 6506 ⓛ 08.45–16.45 daily ⓘ Admission charge; check with the tourist board for battle dates

Historic St Augustine

In the collection of tiny narrow streets at the heart of the modern town you are transported back in time to 18th-century St Augustine. The Gonzáles-Alvarez House claims to be the oldest in the town and is open as a museum. Head to traffic-free St George Street where you will find residents dressed in Spanish costumes waiting to give you the low-down on life as a settler in the 1600s, and you can watch artisans at work in the Spanish Quarter.
ⓐ St George Street ⓛ All historic St Augustine museums and attractions open 09.00–17.00 daily ⓘ Admission charge for Gonzáles-Alvarez House and the Spanish Quarter

Lightner Museum

This intriguing museum houses the vast collections of *objets d'art* accumulated by newspaper magnate Otto C Lightner.

ⓐ 75 King Street ⓣ 904 824 2874 ⓛ 09.00–17.00 daily
ⓦ www.lightnermuseum.org ⓘ Admission charge

St Augustine Sightseeing Trains

Let the train take the strain on this hour-long journey, as you travel past the important historic monuments.

ⓣ 904 829 6545 or 800 226 6545 (freephone in US)

◔ *Castillo de San Marcos*

EXCURSIONS

St Petersburg

Sitting on the south-western coast of Tampa Bay, St Petersburg is quite a contrast to both Orlando and St Augustine in atmosphere. St Petersburg has world-class art museums and an interesting history.

THINGS TO SEE & DO

Museum of Fine Arts

A surprisingly rich collection of European, American, Greek and Roman as well as renowned pre-Columbian and Asian art.

ⓐ 255 Beach Drive NE, near **The Pier** ⓣ 727 896 2667
ⓦ www.fine-arts.org ⓛ 10.00–17.00 Tues–Sat, 13.00–17.00 Sun
ⓘ Admission charge

The Pier

Tourists flock to this long pier for the shopping (there's a five-storey mall at the eastern end), fishing (rent gear) and pelican feeding.

ⓐ 800 2nd Avenue NE ⓣ 727 821 6443 ⓛ 10.00–21.00 Mon–Thur, 10.00–22.00 Fri & Sat, 11.00–19.00 Sun

Salvador Dalí Museum

One of the world's largest collections of the Spanish surrealist's paintings.

ⓐ 1000 3rd Street South ⓣ 727 823 3767 or 800 442 3254 (freephone in US) ⓦ www.salvadordalimuseum.org ⓛ 09.30–17.30 Mon–Wed, Fri & Sat, 09.30–20.00 Thur, 12.00–17.30 Sun ⓘ Admission charge

St Petersburg Historical and Flight One Museum

The world's first scheduled passenger flight took place from St Petersburg's lovely airport. This small museum commemorates that.

ⓐ 335 North Second Avenue ⓣ 727 894 1052 ⓛ 12.00–19.00 Mon, 10.00–17.00 Tues–Sat, 12.00–17.00 Sun ⓘ Admission charge

ⓞ *Surfing the waves*

LIFESTYLE
The American way

Food & drink

Eating is one of the great pleasures of a trip to Orlando. It is difficult
to walk more than a few yards without passing an opportunity to
grab some fast food, or indulge in a full meal with table service.

WHEN TO EAT

You can take breakfast from around 07.00 and this can be anything
from Continental-style (often provided at hotels), to vast 'eat all you
want' buffets of hot and cold dishes. Americans love to 'brunch' and you
can eat this as late as 11.00.

Lunch is served in the middle of the day and many restaurants that
are more formal will have set hours (11.00–15.00).

Americans generally eat dinner early and restaurants are often at
their busiest between 18.00–19.30. Don't worry if you want to eat later,
most places stay open until 22.00 and later at weekends.

PROTOCOL

Most restaurants will ask you to wait to be seated. This is so that each
of the waiting staff has a balanced workload. You may have the choice
of a smoking or non-smoking table, although many restaurants no
longer have smoking areas. Don't forget to tip! Fifteen per cent of the
bill is normal.

Family-oriented restaurants will often have a 'one child eats free with
each adult' policy, and 'early bird' specials also save money (eat dinner
before 18.00).

FAST FOOD & SNACKS

America was the birthplace of the fast-food revolution, so it is not
surprising that you will find as many snack joints as formal restaurants.
You can eat on the move or sit at dinette seats. Choose from burgers,
pizza, sandwiches, bagels, ice cream, churros (sweet fried fritters)
or popcorn.

WHAT TO EAT

There is no end of choice as far as 'good ole' American cuisine is concerned. Steaks come in all shapes and sizes, from junior to Homer Simpson size. Barbecued chicken and ribs are another juicy alternative.

Orlando is not far from the sea in any direction and seafood is abundant, fresh and delicious. Local fish, including grouper, dolphin fish (not the loveable sea mammal, but a large fish also called mahi mahi or dorado) and wahoo, form the basis of many dishes; or try the snow crabs, shrimps or fresh imported lobster.

The cultural mix of Florida means that the world is available on a plate. There is a choice of Caribbean-style spicy foods, Chinese and Thai dishes, Cuban, Mexican and familiar old Italian recipes.

DRINKS

Coffee and tea are available everywhere, hot or iced, and many family restaurants will give you as many free refills as you can take.

Soda (pop) is the drink of choice for most Americans, with Coke and Pepsi the main cola brand names. Florida is famous for its fresh orange juice and you can order this at most establishments. Smoothies are widely available and are very refreshing on a hot day.

ALCOHOL

American beer is of the light lager variety, served ice-cold. It is cheapest on draught, as in the UK, but you can get it in bottles. Smaller breweries make darker, more fully flavoured beers so do ask your server for advice if you want something with a little more bite.

Wine is readily available and mostly Californian, though Australian, Chilean and French wines are easy to locate as well. Americans sometimes call rosé wine 'blush'.

Remember: the legal age to consume alcohol is 21. Bars and clubs are strict and staff may ask for photographic ID before entry: carry your passport, even if you are well above the legal age. Drink driving rules are strictly enforced, and one beer, glass of wine or cocktail puts you at the legal limit.

Menu decoder

GENERAL

Appetiser Starter
Broiled Grilled
Entrée Main course
Grilled Flame grilled
Place setting/silverware Cutlery

BREAKFAST

Biscuit Savoury scone
Eggs 'over easy' Eggs fried both sides but still soft
Eggs 'sunny side up' Eggs fried only on one side
Grits Ground boiled corn, like savoury porridge but stiffer
Hash browns Grated potato, fried
Jelly Jam

OTHER FOOD THAT MAY CONFUSE YOU

Chips Crisps
Chowder A thick soup
Conch (pronounced 'conk') Marine sea snail (more delicious than you can imagine)
Cookie Biscuit
French fries Chips
Liquor Spirits (gin, whisky etc)
Shot Measure
Shrimp Prawn

Portions are gargantuan by British standards. Consider splitting the main course with a friend or spouse, even if a small fee applies. And don't be shy to ask for any leftover food to be packed up for you to take with you if you want to eat it later (in a 'doggie bag'); it is a common practice.

Shopping

Retail therapy is one of the major attractions of a trip to Orlando. Americans know how to make shopping fun and easy with shops being open from 10.00 until at least 21.00 every day except Sunday.

WHAT TO BUY

Branded goods are the must-buy items. Clothing is the most popular, from top American high-street brands including Banana Republic, Timberland, Tommy Hilfiger, Gap and Levi's. There is an abundance of sportswear by all the big names, from trainers to shorts and shirts.

Be aware that videos may not play on your machine back home. DVDs certainly won't unless you have a Region 1 or region-free player. Electrical goods run on 110 volts in the US and so will not work in the UK without a transformer, though most notebook computers come with transformers; all you need to do on return is change the lead to have a British plug. Add 6 per cent to all ticket prices. This is Florida state tax.

WHERE TO SHOP

Most of the malls close to the main tourist areas are outlet malls, with substantial savings even on normal American prices. **Prime Outlets Orlando**, at the northern tip of I-Drive, is the largest outlet mall in the area; it has more than 170 stores with well-known brand names (see page 25). **Florida Outlet Mall** in Lake Buena Vista is more upmarket with names such as Giorgio Armani and MaxMara.

Normal malls still offer good value and perhaps a better range of goods. The nearest to the tourist centres is **Florida Mall** on Sand Lake Drive intersection with Orange Blossom Trail, out to the east (☎ 407 851 6255).

I-Drive has its own stores, often selling souvenir Disney characters cheaper than at the attractions themselves, although the quality is not always as good. **Pointe Orlando** is where you can find more well-known brand names (see page 25).

Some of the best shops are at Disney and Universal, but there are also good stores at Jungleland, Gatorland® and Busch Gardens®.

Children

Orlando is kid heaven. Where else could you spend up to two weeks in a total fantasy world, get up close with dolphins, play all day on water slides or stare into the jaws of an alligator? It is not just the attractions either. Because children form a large percentage of Orlando's visitors, they are made to feel at home right across the resort.

EVENING SHOWS

Where most resorts might pack the kids off to bed early, Orlando offers them a wealth of exciting evening shows where they can cheer the 'goodies' and boo the 'baddies'. Best for small children is **Pirate's Dinner Adventure** (see page 23) – almost like a panto with plenty of opportunities for the kids to get involved. Older children will love the horse show at **Arabian Nights** (see page 34) while teenagers might go for **Medieval Times** (see page 34) with lots of knights and swordfights.

THEME PARKS

If you have very young children, **Magic Kingdom® Park** is where you can easily spend a lot of time without fighting boredom. If you have teenagers, head for **Universal Studios** or **Epcot®**. In general, the other parks, from **Islands of Adventure®** to **Disney's Animal Kingdom® Park** and **Disney's Hollywood™ Studios**, have a very broad appeal for all age groups, as do **SeaWorld®** and **Busch Gardens®**. **Silver Springs®** has very good animal exhibits but no roller coasters.

Rent a pushchair (stroller) at all the major parks because you will probably find that even the most active child will become tired after a few hours in a theme park.

WATER PARKS

This is a good way to cool down and have fun. **Wet 'n Wild®** (see page 19) is an excellent park, and Disney has several for you to choose from.

Sports & activities

AIRBOAT RIDES

Ride out over the swamplands to see how Florida looked fewer than 30 years ago with **Boggy Creek Airboat Rides**. See alligators, turtles and a range of bird life in their natural habitat. Boggy Creek also operate night-time alligator viewing trips with advance booking, and parasailing on the freshwater lake beyond a 'gator's range (you don't get wet unless you want to). ⓐ Boggy Creek Rd (Orlando Airport area) ⓣ 407 344 9550 ⓦ www.bcairboats.com ⓛ 09.00–17.30 daily, rides every 45 minutes

BALLOON RIDES

One of the best ways to get a panoramic view over Orlando and the surrounding area is from a balloon. The conditions are best in the early morning because there is little or no wind, and you will meet for your briefing before dawn. Flights last around an hour, after which you are welcomed into the ballooning fraternity with a glass of champagne before enjoying a buffet breakfast.
Orange Blossom Balloons ⓣ 407 239 7677 ⓛ Flights daily ⓘ Admission fee and hotel transfers for a small extra fee

● *Splash around and cool down*

LIFESTYLE

GOLF

With almost 200 golf courses and a near-perfect climate, it's no wonder that many holiday-makers choose to take to the tee in central Florida. Some of the higher-class hotels have been quick to add courses and even Disney has realised there is a market for adults on the greens when the kids are at the theme parks.

The officially endorsed PGA Guide to Golf produces a complimentary magazine full of information and details of public golf courses in Orlando. This is distributed at tourist information centres across the Orlando/ Daytona area or get further information at (W) www.pgatour.com).

Festivals & events

It seems that Orlando is like one long festival. However, theme park 'imagineers' (show, parade and set designers) pull out all the stops with extra special activities added to the already full programmes for major American holidays. The main three are Independence Day (4 July), Thanksgiving (fourth Thursday in November) and Christmas. Americans call late December 'the holidays' because the period covers a time of celebration for other faiths as well as Christians. Disney parades become a riot of even more twinkling lights and Santa Claus spends time finding out just what every little girl or boy wants.

The east coast of Florida has a number of seasonal events. Spring Break is the traditional time when students leave their books and head for the coast, and Cocoa Beach and Daytona are popular destinations. Events include volleyball, surfing and 'chilling out'.

Daytona holds racing events throughout the year, but the major meets are the Daytona 500 and the Daytona 200, usually held in March. Race fans make up a proportion of the visitors, but these events also attract thousands of bikers from around America. There is also another 'fest' in late October or early November.

▶ *The distinctive yellow taxi cabs of America*

Accommodation

Price rating

Hotels in Florida are graded according to a star system running from one star for a cheap hostel to five stars for a luxurious resort with numerous facilities. The ratings in this book are as follows:

£ = up to $120   ££ = $121–$200   £££ = over $200

All prices are the cost per night for two people staying in a double room.

INTERNATIONAL DRIVE

Fairfield Inn & Suites International Drive £–££ Motel-style rooms that offer a clean and comfortable place to rest your head. Go for value. ⓐ 7495 Canada Avenue ⓣ 407 351 7000 Ⓦ www.fairfieldinn.com

Peabody Orlando ££–£££ Elegant property catering to a mostly business and convention crowd. Be sure to stick around to see the gaggle of five mallard ducks that trot through the lobby every morning and evening. ⓐ 9801 International Drive ⓣ 407 352 4000 Ⓦ www.peabodyorlando.com

LAKE BUENA VISTA

Hotel Royal Plaza £–££ Nice-sized rooms in a property well known for its service levels. The hotel is one of the oldest in the area, but has recently emerged from a vast renovation. ⓐ 1905 Hotel Plaza Boulevard ⓣ 407 828 2828 Ⓦ www.royalplaza.com

Buena Vista Palace £–£££ Comfortable hotel suitable for business or leisure. The location near Downtown Disney® makes it suitable for adults or those travelling with older children. ⓐ 1900 Buena Vista Drive ⓣ 407 827 3278 Ⓦ www.buenavistapalace.com

KISSIMMEE

Comfort Suites Maingate East ££ Two pools, large rooms and convenient access to a shopping centre and mini-golf course keep young and

old happy at this great-value hotel. ⓐ 2775 Florida Plaza Boulevard
ⓣ 407 397 7848 ⓦ www.comfortsuitesfl.com

Renaissance Orlando Resort at SeaWorld® ££–£££ This well-appointed
property located across the street from SeaWorld® recently emerged
from a huge renovation which saw the addition of a full-service spa.
ⓐ 6677 Sea Harbor Drive ⓣ 407 351 5555
ⓦ www.renaissanceseaworld.com

The Omni at ChampionsGate £££ When Disney begins to pall, this
resort steps in to keep guests thoroughly occupied. Play golf on
the championship golf course designed by Greg Norman, enjoy the
pool area complete with lazy river, or relax at the spa.
ⓐ 8390 ChampionsGate Boulevard ⓣ 407 390 6664
ⓦ www.omnihotels.com

CELEBRATION
Celebration Hotel £££ Built in the same style as the planned community
that it's surrounded by, the Celebration Hotel is a thoroughly romantic
choice for couples. Rooms overlook the lake or marketplace – and the
entire property is stuffed with antiques and charm. ⓐ 700 Bloom Street
ⓣ 407 566 6000 ⓦ www.celebrationhotel.com.

DISNEY WORLD RESORT
Disney's All-Star Music Resort £–££ Value-priced resort on Disney
property. Guests benefit from a number of extras – like early entry to the
parks. Rooms tend to be on the small side. ⓐ 1701 W. Buena Vista Drive
ⓣ 407 934 7639 ⓦ www.disneyworld.com

Disney's Grand Floridian £££ Faux-Victorian resort that adds a touch
of elegance to Disney's standard hotel offerings. Couples and
honeymooners especially love the romantic touches – including crystal
chandeliers and a fantastic spa. ⓐ 4401 Floridian Way ⓣ 407 934 7639
ⓦ www.disneyworld.com

Preparing to go

GETTING THERE
By air
The largest airport with international airlinks in Orlando is Orlando International Airport. Orlando-Sanford is also offered as a destination by charter airlines. Tampa, Fort Lauderdale and Miami also have international airports that may prove convenient for long-stay holiday-makers. The average flying time non-stop to Orlando from London is 9 hours, or 2.5 hours from New York.

Many people are aware that air travel emits CO_2, which contributes to climate change. You may be interested in the possibility of lessening the environmental impact of your flight through the charity Climate Care, which offsets your CO_2 by funding environmental projects around the world. Visit Ⓦ www.climatecare.org

TOURIST INFORMATION
VisitFlorida is Florida's state tourism agency with offices in the United Kingdom. There is also a good website offering tips and advice at Ⓦ www.visitflorida.com. You can request maps and vacation guides by filling out the online request forms on this site.

BEFORE YOU LEAVE
Health & prescriptions Take regular prescription medicines with you to ensure you don't run out. Pack a small first-aid kit with plasters, antiseptic cream, travel sickness pills, insect repellent and bite-relief creams, upset stomach remedies, painkillers and protective sun creams. Consider a dental check before you go if you are planning an extended stay. Ask your hotel receptionist or your tour operator rep to recommend a doctor or dentist in the event of an emergency.

Insurance Check that your insurance policy covers you adequately for loss of possessions and valuables, for activities you might want to try – say horse riding or water sports – and for emergency medical and dental treatment, including flights home, if required.

Security Take precautions to ensure that your house does not get burgled when you are away. Cancel regular deliveries and let your local postal delivery person know where they can leave any bulk packages. If possible, arrange for a friend or neighbour to drop into the house regularly and leave signs of activity (such as opening and closing curtains and turning lights on and off). Check your burglar alarm is working and is switched on (your insurance policy may require this). Leave the code and house keys with a trustworthy friend or neighbour in case of emergencies.

ENTRY FORMALITIES

Visitors to the United States who are citizens of the UK, the Irish Republic, Australia and New Zealand will need a machine-readable passport for stays of up to 90 days and a return airline ticket. They will also need to fill out a green visa waiver form, which is usually distributed on board the plane prior to arrival. South Africans will need to apply for a visa through the American Embassy in their country of residence. Canadians only need to present a passport for entry to the United States. No visa or visa waiver is required.

MONEY

The currency in the United States is the dollar (USD, $). You can withdraw money using ATMs at most American banks. Make sure you know your PIN and check with your bank to see if there are any charges for using your card abroad; at present Nationwide is the only UK bank offering free ATM transactions abroad. US banks do not really have foreign exchange facilities. Instead, you will need to change money at foreign exchange offices, which can be easily found in tourist areas. The most widely accepted credit cards are Visa, American Express and MasterCard.

CLIMATE

Florida has a tropical climate. If you travel between October and May, expect showers (some heavy) and occasional chilly spells, though the temperature rarely drops below 15°C (60°F) and will reach 27–28°C (the low 80s°F) during the day. In summer, you may still encounter afternoon downpours, but the temperatures are generally around 30–32°C (the high 80s°F) and the nights are warm.

Hurricane season is from June to October. While these storms are well-predicted and generally only a minor inconvenience to holiday-makers, hurricanes are deadly and warnings should be heeded.

At all times of year, the atmosphere can be very humid as the rain evaporates. The sun will be very hot, so take plenty of sun protection, a hat and sunglasses for each member of the family.

BAGGAGE ALLOWANCE

Baggage allowances vary according to the airline, destination and the class of travel, but 20 kg (44 lb) per person is the norm for luggage that is carried in the hold. You are generally allowed one item of cabin baggage weighing no more than 5 kg (11 lb), and measuring 46 by 30 by 23 cm (18 by 12 by 9 inches), although rules at different airports vary, so it is best to check with your airline before you go if you are in any doubt about what you can take. Large items – surfboards, golf clubs and pushchairs – are usually charged as extras and it is worth notifying the airline in advance if you want to bring these. Be sure to limit your carry-on liquids as you can only bring liquids on board in a small, clear, sealable plastic bag in containers of no more than 100 ml (3½ fl oz).

During your stay

AIRPORTS

Orlando has two airports: Orlando International is south-east of the city and handles scheduled and some holiday charter flights, while Orlando-Sanford airport is 48 km (30 miles) north-east of the city and deals only with holiday flights. Before you enter the United States, you'll be asked to complete a customs form and you will not be allowed to take any raw foods into the country. Duty-free limits for entry are one litre of spirits or wine (travellers must be over 21), 210 cigarettes or 100 cigars (not Cuban) and up to $100 (about £200) worth of gifts.

If you are travelling with a tour operator, you will be met by a rep outside the Arrivals terminal. Fly/drive passengers will find the major car hire companies within the Arrivals terminal at Orlando International and just across the road from the Arrivals terminal at Orlando-Sanford.

COMMUNICATIONS
Phones

International SIM cards usually work in the US but charge huge fees – usually about £1 a minute. A better option is to purchase a local SIM card, which charges about a third of the cost for international calls. Local calls are easy to dial – just ring the number, making sure to drop the prefix area code. Making long-distance calls in the US and Canada will require you to dial 1 plus a three-digit area code, followed by the seven-digit number.

> ### TELEPHONING ABROAD
> To make an international call, dial the international code (011), followed by the country code, the area code and then the number. The country code for Australia is +61, for the UK +44, for the Irish Republic +353, for South Africa +27 and for New Zealand +64.

Public phones tend to be placed at busy intersections. As a result, it can be a challenge hearing anything that is being said down the line. The minimum charge for a local call is 25 cents.

Post

The US Postal Service offers a reliable and speedy service, but there are not many offices in tourist areas. If you only want to send a postcard, it's much easier to buy stamps from local shops or supermarkets and post them at your hotel. Postboxes are blue and referred to as mailboxes in America.

Internet

Internet access is widespread across the country; however, connection speeds may be slower and costs higher than you are used to. Internet cafés are not common; however, most hotels will offer a business centre, in-room access and WiFi. Prices in hotels are on the high side, costing anything between US$2 and US$4 per hour.

CUSTOMS

English is the native tongue of Florida. You may also find a number of fluent Spanish speakers due to the large Hispanic population in the state.

The United States tends to be conservative when it comes to lifestyles. There are also some elements of racism, sexism and homophobia in some cultures; however, many companies are doing their best to erase these elements from American society.

Women should feel comfortable travelling around Orlando after dark; however, they may not want to travel through non-touristy communities or in the city centre. If in doubt, try and travel with a friend when going through unfamiliar neighbourhoods.

If you are using public transport or passing someone in the street, then always give way to the elderly and mothers with children.

When conversing, Americans are friendly and gregarious. They may tell you all about their personal worries and even their exact salary level – but shy away from sexual and political topics due to a fear that they are too 'vulgar'.

Service in shops and restaurants is very efficient – sometimes to the point of annoyance. Salespeople will always be available to help with a smile in order to close the sale.

DRESS CODES

When travelling around Florida, casual shorts and t-shirts are the norm. Bathing suits are fine near the pool or at the beach; however, thong bikinis and Speedos are generally frowned upon.

The only time you will need to dress conservatively is when you plan on eating out at a fine dining establishment. Some five-star hotels may also have dress codes after a certain time in the evening.

ELECTRICITY

American electrical voltage is 110 volts and electrical items such as hairdryers and shavers you bring from home will be a little slower or less powerful. You'll need an adapter plug with two flat pins to fit an American electrical socket. If you are buying electrical appliances to take home, always check that they will work in the UK before purchasing them.

EMERGENCIES

EMERGENCY NUMBERS
Ambulance, fire brigade (fire department) and police 911

GETTING AROUND
Driving

Americans drive on the right. Speed limits are signposted on the roadside and alter frequently, so keep your eyes on them.

Traffic is controlled more by traffic lights at intersections than roundabouts. Traffic can turn right at a red light after first coming to a complete stop, unless signs say it is forbidden (watch out for people crossing the road before you do).

Road names are hung above the intersection. The name you can read is that of the road you are crossing – and not of the road you are on. Do not overtake yellow school buses when they are flashing their lights. When they stop, so must you – even when you are on the other side of the road.

When on dual carriageways, cars can pass on either side and some exits are on the left of the carriageway.

Do not drink and drive: There are serious penalties even for a first-time offender and one drink of beer, wine or cocktail will put you at the legal limit.

Always carry your driving licence and car hire papers when you are driving the car in case you are stopped by police – and if you are stopped by police, do not get out of the car. Instead, put your hands on the steering wheel until advised otherwise by an officer. Note that car stops are the single most dangerous aspect of American police work, so officers (who are all armed) are highly alert when they approach a stopped car.

If another motorist signals that there is something wrong with your car, or nudges the back of your car, do not stop straight away. Drive to a public place such as a petrol station just in case it's a hoax.

If you have an accident, the police must be called before you move your car. Your car hire firm should give you a number to call in case of a breakdown. If you are on a major highway, raise the bonnet of your car and a passing police patrol will offer assistance. Dial 911 if it's an emergency.

Pay particular attention to local parking restrictions. Do not park within 3 m (10 ft) of a fire hydrant or lowered kerb. Most restaurants and shops have ample parking. Park bonnet-first so that the registration tag, on the rear, can be seen. Do not park against the direction of traffic or you will be ticketed.

Driving vocabulary is different from the UK:

US	UK
Gas	Petrol
Gas pedal	Accelerator
Trunk	Car boot
Hood	Car bonnet
Fender	Car bumper

Windshield	Windscreen
Freeway	Motorway
No standing	No parking or stopping
Ramp	Slip road
Yield	Give way
Downtown	City centre

Car hire

Car hire is easy in Orlando and – at first glance – prices are cheap. You should note that basic costs do not include insurance, taxes and other surcharges. These can more than double the final bill. Don't accept the fuel purchase option – touted as a money saver – unless you're positive you can return the car running on fumes. Choose to return the car with a full tank of gas, then make sure it's actually full before returning it otherwise you'll have to shell out up to $5 a gallon for the tank to be filled onsite. Packages bought in the UK will often include all these extras, so it's worth while shopping around. Make sure that you have Collision Damage Waiver (CDW), also known as Loss Damage Waiver (LDW), which will cover you for any damage to the car, whatever the cause. Liability or Extended Protection covers you in case you cause an accident – important in litigation-crazy America.

Local and international rental companies include:

Avis Ⓦ www.avis.com

Hertz Ⓦ www.hertz.com

Public transport

The Lynx bus system operates throughout the Orlando metropolitan area. They can be contacted by phone (Ⓣ 407 841 5969) or on the web (Ⓦ www.golynx.com). The main routes (or lines) that are helpful to visitors are 56 (Highway 192 in Kissimmee to the Magic Kingdom® Park) and 50 (I-Drive to the Magic Kingdom® Park). Generally, there is one bus every 30 minutes and ticket prices are cheap.

I-Drive has its own trolleybus service called I-Ride running along its 9.5 km (6 mile) length and along Universal Boulevard running parallel to

I-Drive to the east. It runs from 07.00 to 23.30 at 15-minute intervals. Prices are cheap but have plenty of coins ready as the correct fare is needed. Day passes for up to 14 days are available. They can be contacted on phone (☎ 407 248 9590) or on the web (Ⓦ www.iridetrolley.com).

HEALTH, SAFETY & CRIME
Healthcare
It is not necessary to take any special health precautions or have any vaccinations prior to travelling to the United States. Tap water is safe to drink; however, the taste may not to be your liking as it can be heavily chlorinated. Bottled water is becoming more popular as an option.

Florida has the unhappy distinction of being a state whose population has an extremely high proportion of people living with HIV. Condoms are therefore a must. They are available in most convenience stores and pharmacies.

Heatstroke is a common problem, so don't go anywhere without appropriate clothing and ample water supplies. A hat and plenty of sunscreen are vital.

Pharmacies are prevalent pretty much everywhere; however, you will need a prescription for any pharmaceuticals. If in doubt, ask your doctor to provide you with a prescription before you depart on holiday. Getting a doctor to fill out a prescription in America can be extremely expensive.

Facilities for emergency treatment are very good, with a number of private hospitals in the area. Dentists are very well qualified, but you'll have to pay and claim back from your insurance company after you return to your home country. Dial 911 in cases of emergency.

Valuables, crime & the police
Serious crime against tourists is rare, but you can minimise your chances of becoming a victim by taking the following precautions:
- Don't carry large amounts of cash and don't flash cash around when you buy things in shops. Pay with a credit card where possible and keep your card in a safe place.
- Leave all valuables such as plane tickets, extra traveller's cheques and

cash in the hotel safe. You may have to pay a small daily charge to use this, but the peace of mind is worth it.

- Don't leave bags lying around at cafés and nightspots.
- Take all valuables out of the car whenever you leave it. See section on driving (page 118) for other security advice.
- Don't open your hotel door to strangers and don't invite people back to your room.
- If you become a victim of a crime, don't put up a fight as the criminals may be armed. Dial 911 for the police.
- You will need a police report if you want to claim on your insurance for any missing money or property. If you are given the original of this form, rather than a photocopy, hang on to it and take photocopies to give anyone who requests one.

MEDIA
Newspapers
Orlando newspapers tend to be extremely local in view. Coverage of African rioting or Asian landslides will be ignored in favour of the crowning of the latest Orange Queen at the county fair. The local paper of choice is the *Orlando Sentinel* – a good publication for local events and attraction information, yet less impressive if you're looking to stay in touch with the outside world. For national coverage, *USA Today* and the *Wall Street Journal* offer alternatives; however, *USA Today* is extremely tabloid in style, while the *Wall Street Journal* focuses on financial news.

For international coverage, your best bet is to stick to online British publications.

Television
There are four major networks showcasing the 'best' in American drama and comedy in the United States: NBC, CBS, ABC and Fox. Many hotels also subscribe to cable networks such as CNN (all news) and HBO (edgier drama such as *Sex and the City* and *Six Feet Under*). News broadcasts on television tend to be extremely local with limited international coverage. One major exception is *60 Minutes*, broadcast every Sunday evening on

CBS. BBC World and BBC America are also commonly available, allowing UK visitors to stay in touch with home.

Radio

There are dozens of radio stations in Orlando playing everything from jazz and blues to country to rock. There are also a number of all-talk stations specialising in news, format and debate programming. For high culture, dial in to NPR (National Public Radio), similar in style to Radio 4. Programming at American radio stations is highly structured, meaning that you may hear the same song dozens of times in a single day. You'll also hear lots of advertisements scattered between almost every song and news update.

OPENING HOURS

Banks Open Monday–Friday 09.00–15.00, and some on Saturday 09.00–13.00, but there are numerous 24-hour ATM machines where you can withdraw cash on a Cirrus, NYCE or credit card. Most establishments also accept travellers' cheques in payment – although these are decreasing in usage globally due to the ease and convenience of internationally recognised debit cards. Note that foreign currency exchange is not a standard service in American banks.

Museums and attractions Cultural institutions are open daily from 09.00 to 17.00; however, tourist attractions keep longer hours. Theme parks (depending on the season) stay open from 09.00 to midnight.

Shops In the tourist areas, shops open around 10.00 and stay open until 22.00, though shops in non-tourist areas open Monday–Saturday 10.00–21.00 and 11.00-20.00 on Sundays. Pharmacies are open during the same times as other shops, but there will also always be a 24-hour pharmacy open somewhere in the local community.

RELIGION

America is a predominantly Christian country with many denominations. Masses and services are held on Sundays (some denominations on Saturdays). Your hotel will have details of the closest churches to you. Sizable Muslim and Jewish populations also live in Florida. Your concierge should have details of local mosques and synagogues.

TIME DIFFERENCES

Orlando is situated in the Eastern Standard Time zone, five hours behind London (GMT). During North American Daylight Saving at noon in Orlando, time at home is as follows:

Australia Eastern Standard Time 22.00, Central Standard Time 21.30, Western Standard Time 21.00

New Zealand 01.00 (next day)

South Africa 14.00

UK and Republic of Ireland 17.00

US and Canada Newfoundland Time 13.30, Atlantic Canada Time 13.00, Eastern Standard Time 12.00, Central Time 11.00, Mountain Time 10.00, Pacific Time 09.00, Alaska 08.00

TIPPING

As a basic guide, leave 15 per cent at restaurants and offer the same to taxi and limo drivers. Room cleaners should be given $1 a day per occupant, while bellboys should be given $1 a bag. When in a bar, add $1 per drink to each order to give to the bartender.

TOILETS

All major attractions are well kitted out with toilet facilities. Shopping centres will also have facilities, many with baby-changing rooms and family-friendly amenities. When you want to know where the public toilets are, ask for the bathroom or restroom as the word toilet is considered vulgar.

TRAVELLERS WITH DISABILITIES

In the US, all businesses that deal with the public, including hotels, attractions and restaurants, are required by law to have facilities for people with disabilities. In Orlando, International Drive has lowered kerbs at all crossing points and intersections to allow for easier road crossing and the theme parks have designated routes for visitors with disabilities. Most shops and restaurants have parking bays for disabled drivers. A British disabled parking badge will be recognised in the US, so if you have one, bring it with you. Individual rides in the theme parks will have differing rules, so enquire with the parks themselves about restrictions.

Ⓦ www.sath.org (US-based site)

Ⓦ www.access-able.com (general advice on worldwide travel)

Ⓦ http://travel.guardian.co.uk (UK site offering tips and links for disabled travellers)

A

accommodation 110–11
Adventureland® 43
air travel 112, 114, 115
airboat rides 29, 107
alcohol 103, 115, 118
Aquatica® 8, 73
ATMs 113, 122

B

baggage allowances 114
balloon rides 107
banks 122
beach resorts 88–90
boat trips 63, 70, 96, 97
Busch Gardens® 83–7
buses and trolleybuses 119–20

C

car hire 119
Celebration 37–9, 111
children 106
cinemas 22, 23, 39
Cirque du Soleil® 56
classic bikes and cars 30–1
Clearwater 89
climate 8, 113–14
Cocoa Beach 89, 108
credit cards 113, 120
crime 120–1
customs, American 116–17

D

Daytona Beach 10, 89–90, 108
dinner shows 23, 24, 34, 106
disabilities, travellers with 123–4
Discovery Cove® 10, 77–80
DisneyQuest® Indoor Interactive
    Theme Park 56
Disney's Animal Kingdom® Park
    50–1
Disney's Blizzard Beach Water Park
    54
Disney's Hollywood™ Studios 10,
    52–3

Disney's Typhoon Lagoon 54
Disney's Wide World of Sports®
    Complex 54–5
Dolphin Swim 80
Downtown Disney® 10, 56–8
dress codes 117
drinking water 41, 120
driving 103, 117–19
duty-free allowances 115

E

electricity 117
emergency numbers 117
Epcot® 10, 46–9

F

Fantasy of Flight 91
Fantasyland 43
festivals and events 108
firework displays 23, 45, 49
fishing 89, 100
Flying Tigers Warbird Air Restoration
    Museum 29–30
food and drink 102–4
Frontierland 43
Future World 47–8

G

Gatorland® 11, 30
golf and adventure golf 15, 17, 26, 29,
    35, 108, 111
Green Meadows Farm 35

H

Harry P Leu Formal Gardens 15
healthcare 112, 120
heatstroke 120
helicopter tours 15–16, 29, 30

I

insurance 112
International Drive (I-Drive) 14–25,
    110, 119–20
Internet access 116
Islands of Adventure® 59, 65–70

J

Jurassic Park® 65

K

Kissimmee 28–36, 110–11

L

Lake Buena Vista 26–7, 110
Lost Continent® 66

M

Magic Kingdom® Park 8, 11, 42–5
magic show 23
Magical Midway 16–17
Main Street, USA® 44
Maingate 35–6
Marvel Super Hero Island® 66, 68
medical treatment 112, 120
money 113
motor racing 89–90, 108

N

NASA Kennedy Space Center 11, 92–5
newspapers 121
nightlife see individual locations

O

opening hours 122
Orlando Science Center 17

P

parades 44, 51, 52, 108
passports and visas 113
pharmacies 120, 122
phones 115–16
postal service 116

R

radio 122
religious services 122–3
Reptile World Serpentarium 31
restaurants and bars see individual
    locations
Richard Petty Driving Experience 55,
    90

Ripley's Believe It or Not!®
    Odditorium 17

S

St Augustine 98–9
St Petersburg 100
SeaWorld® 11, 23, 73–6
Seuss Landing™ 68
Shamu Stadium 75
shopping 8, 105, 122
    see also individual locations
Silver Springs 96–7
Skull Kingdom 19
SkyCoaster® 32
SkyVenture® 19
Space Shuttle launches 95
surfing 89

T

television 121–2
time differences 123
tipping 102, 123
Titanic Ship of Dreams – The
    Exhibition 19
toilets 123
Tomorrowland 44
Toon Lagoon® 69–70
tourist information 112
Twilight Zone Tower of Terror™ 10, 52

U

Universal CityWalk® 59, 71–2
Universal Orlando® Resort 59–72
Universal Studios Florida® 11, 59,
    60–4

W

Walt Disney World® Resort 40–58,
    111
water parks 19–20, 54, 106
Wet 'n Wild® 19–20
women travellers 116
WonderWorks 20–1
World of Orchids 35
World Showcase 48–9

FIND THE LATEST HOTSPOT

Get more from your holiday and discover the best restaurants, bars, beaches and family-friendly attractions with these handy pocket guides. Our wide range covers over 45 destinations:

Algarve
Bali
Brazil
Bulgaria:
  Black Sea Resorts
Corfu
Corsica
Costa Blanca
Costa Brava &
Costa Dorada
Costa del Sol &
Costa de Almeria
Côte D'Azur
Crete
Croatia
Cuba
Cyprus
Dominican Republic
Egypt:
  Red Sea Resorts
Fuerteventura
Gibraltar
Goa
Gran Canaria
Guernsey
Halkidiki
Hawaii
Ibiza
Ionian Islands

Jamaica
Jersey
Kenya:
  Indian Ocean
  Resorts
Lanzarote
Madeira
Maldives
Mallorca
Malta
Menorca
Mexico
Morocco
Neapolitan Rivier
Orlando
Rhodes & Kos
Santorini
Sardinia
Sicily
Sri Lanka
Tenerife
Thailand
Tunisia
Turkey –
  Aegean Coast
  Lycian Coast
  Mediterranean
  Coast

Available from all good bookshops, your local Thomas Cook travel store or browse and buy on-line at www.thomascookpublishing.com

Thomas Cook
Publishing

ACKNOWLEDGEMENTS

We would like to thank all the photographers, picture libraries and
organisations for the loan of the photographs reproduced in this book,
to whom copyright in the photograph belongs:
Pete Bennett (pages 20, 31, 74, 76, 77, 79, 81, 85, 86, 97, 99, 107); © Disney (pages
42, 45, 47); Andre Jenny/Alamy (page 91); Pictures Colour Library (pages 16, 24,
62, 69); Thomas Cook (pages 59, 67, 93); World Pictures/Photoshot/Disney
(pages 1, 10–11, 46, 51, 55, 57); World Pictures/Photoshot (pages 5, 9, 13, 88, 90,
101, 109)

Project editor: Penny Isaac
Layout: Donna Pedley
Proofreader: Lucilla Watson
Indexer: Marie Lorimer

Send your thoughts to
books@thomascook.com

- Found a beach bar, peaceful stretch of sand or must-see sight that
  we don't feature?

- Like to tip us off about any information that needs a little updating?

- Want to tell us what you love about this handy little guidebook
  and more importantly how we can make it even handier?

Then here's your chance to tell all! Send us ideas, discoveries and
recommendations today and then look out for your valuable input
in the next edition of this title.

Send an email to the above address or write to:
HotSpots Series Editor, Thomas Cook Publishing, PO Box 227,
Unit 9, Coningsby Road, Peterborough PE3 8SB, UK.